Contents

PRIMARY MATHEMATICS SCHEMES
How to choose and use

a Roberts

GHTON
TORONTO

ISBN 0 340 40831 6

First published 1988

Printed and bound in Great Britain for
Hodder and Stoughton Educational,
a division of Hodder and Stoughton Ltd,
Mill Road, Dunton Green, Sevenoaks, Kent,
by The Eastern Press Ltd, Reading

Typeset by Wessex Typesetters
(Division of The Eastern Press Ltd)
Frome, Somerset

Introduction

The last few years have seen a remarkable increase in the number of mathematics schemes available for use in primary schools. Teachers and headteachers are now faced with the kind of decision which they have long had to make in relation to reading schemes. First of all, should they have a scheme or not, and then, if they decide that they do want a scheme, which one will best suit their requirements? The range of schemes now on the market makes this decision difficult and the chief aim of this book is to provide primary school teachers and headteachers with a sound basis on which to make it.

The process of reaching a decision should ideally begin with self analysis and the first part of the book is intended to help teachers to look at themselves, their aspirations and their beliefs about the teaching of mathematics and consider ways in which a scheme might help or hinder them in the achievement of their aims.

The second part consists of a schedule of questions which it is suggested that teachers might usefully ask about a scheme.

In the third part of the book, the significance of the questions is discussed and a variety of currently available schemes is drawn upon to illustrate and be the basis for comment on the kind of answers that may arise. There is no suggestion that this illustrative review should lead to a 'best buy' among the schemes, although it may alert teachers to factors which make some schemes not necessarily better but more suitable for their particular situation than others. The aim is rather to encourage teachers to embark on their own rigorous scrutiny of any scheme which they may contemplate adopting. Such a process might lead to purchase or it might lead to the view that no scheme fulfils sufficient requirements to justify adoption. Whatever the outcome, the decision will be an informed one.

PART ONE

The Contribution of Schemes to the Teaching of Mathematics in the Primary School

1 Introduction

It may be because, as the Cockcroft Committee (1982) declared, 'mathematics is a difficult subject both to teach and to learn' (p. 67), that many teachers lack confidence in their ability to teach it adequately. Particularly vulnerable is the primary school teacher, who is unlikely to have studied mathematics to a very high level (and who may well be female) and therefore have well established feelings of inferiority about the subject (APU, 1981).

In the days when teaching mathematics in primary schools was commonly a matter of training children in the routine skills of computation with occasional consideration of problems concerning moving trains and baths filling up with water, it was not too difficult for the non-specialist teacher to establish an efficient way of working. The broader approach to mathematics conceived of by the 'modern mathematics' movement of the late 1950s and encouraged in primary schools by the first Schools Council Curriculum Bulletin (1965) makes far greater demands on the teacher. Children are expected to arrive at an understanding of the nature of mathematics and its uses through practical experiences, investigation and discussion. Such activities are considerably more difficult to organise and control than the working of computational exercises and consequently the teaching of mathematics has become a far more hazardous process.

The insecurity which many primary school teachers may feel about mathematics can only be deepened by the periodic attacks on mathematics teaching which are mounted with varying degrees of rationality in the press. Indeed, it was as a result of numerous representations to a parliamentary sub-committee, casting doubts on the adequacy and the effectiveness of mathematics teaching that the Cockcroft Committee of Inquiry was set up in 1978. The Committee, in the introduction to their Report, implicitly dissociated such criticism from contemporary teaching approaches with a series of quotations from documents spanning a century. All voiced concern about declining standards in mathematics and served to demonstrate the perennial nature of such fears. Nevertheless, primary school teachers may still find their confidence eroded by such charges.

It is clear then that teachers of mathematics in the primary school are doubly vulnerable. First they are asked to do a complex and demanding job for which they may feel inadequately prepared. Secondly, they are constantly made aware of a state of popular dissatisfaction with the results of their efforts. In this situation it is not surprising that they appear to be turning increasingly to commercially produced materials in the hope that these may offer guidance on the mathematical content of teaching and suggest appropriate activities for the children in their classes. An indication of the extent to which schools have turned to published mathematics schemes may be seen in the remarkable increase during the last ten years in the number of such schemes available.

The decision to adopt a mathematics scheme in a school is understandable but it is not clear on what basis the choice is made. It is one of the most important resolutions a school can make for a step is taken which will fundamentally affect the mathematical life of hundreds of children. Their experience of mathematics is likely to be dominated by the scheme and a wrong choice could condemn them to years of confusion and foster a distaste from which they may never recover.

Once the decision is made, the school is unlikely to be able to afford a change for many years to come, for the investment involved is considerable both in financial terms and in terms of effort on the part of teachers to understand and operate the scheme.

How is such a major decision made? At the

moment, it is likely to depend entirely on the personal efforts of the headteacher and the mathematics coordinator to inform themselves about what is available. There are few sources of independent advice about the range of schemes on offer although some may find local authority specialist advisory staff helpful. Others may be dependent on publishers' promotional literature. Evaluation instruments such as those devised by Harling (1979) and Lumb *et al.* (1984) are useful but difficult for an individual school to apply across a wide range of material.

The aim in this book is two-fold; to help teachers and headteachers to clarify for themselves what they require of a mathematics scheme in their school and to suggest a means of analysing schemes in order to determine which might best fit those requirements. Criteria for forming judgements are proposed and examples of how they might be applied are drawn from a wide range of materials. The intention is that a review of this nature will provide a basis on which teachers can make an informed judgement about the scheme which most closely answers their needs.

Information of this kind can give only partial guidance, however. It cannot be too strongly emphasised that no final decisions should be made until teachers have seen possible schemes at work in schools. Reading about schemes is no substitute for seeing them in action. Things which may seem a good idea on paper may work out differently in practice and direct experience is needed to reveal the way a scheme influences mathematics teaching and learning and the reactions of children and teachers who use it. The wisest course of action would be to examine the schemes according to the suggested criteria in order to narrow the range to a small number of possible schemes and then to observe these in action before making a final choice.

There is no suggestion here that every school should adopt a commercial scheme, but merely an understanding of the reasons why many schools do; teaching mathematics in a primary school today is demanding and can be confusing, and many teachers understandably feel the need of the expert, day-to-day support which they feel a commercial scheme can provide. It may well be that after crystallising what they want a scheme to do for them, teachers may decide that they can do it better themselves. If they do go ahead with their plan to select a scheme, however, it is hoped that this book will help them to make an informed choice which takes account not only of the scheme itself but also of the situation in which it is to be used.

2 The school

The single most important requirement of any commercially produced item, whether it be a simple piece of apparatus or a complete mathematics scheme, is that it should do the job for which it was intended. The first stage in reaching a decision about whether to buy a scheme is therefore to examine the teaching of mathematics in the school and determine the role that a scheme might be expected to play. It is only through an analysis of what a school is attempting to accomplish in its mathematics teaching that a proper analysis can be made of the requirements of a scheme. Above all, the scheme and the teaching must be matched; a scheme prepared on the basis of one set of aspirations and priorities will not work well in a teaching situation founded on different assumptions.

Mathematics is the curriculum area for which a primary school is most likely to have drawn up a scheme of work or guidelines (DES, 1978). This is an indication of the common seriousness with which primary schools approach the task of teaching mathematics, but when that seriousness of approach is translated into action a considerable diversity is apparent. Mathematics as taught in one classroom may bear little resemblance to the same subject in another. This is partly because our state of knowledge

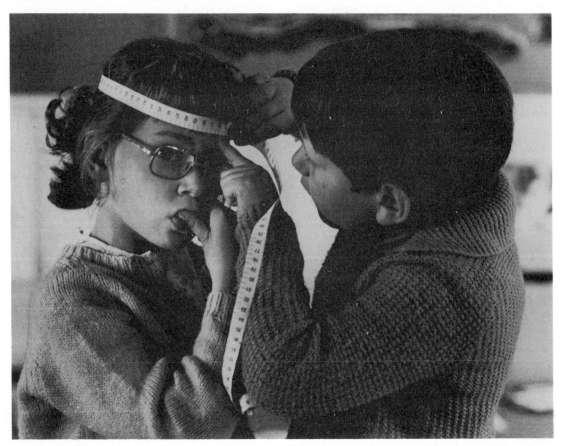

about how children learn mathematics is not such that we can confidently agree upon a single approach to the teaching of it. There is also the question of individual differences among children, teachers and schools which precludes the possibility of agreeing upon one right way of doing things: children and teachers differ in their knowledge and ability and in their preferred ways of working; schools differ in their general aims and the facilities they have for achieving these.

This diversity does not mean that there is no agreement about aims, methods and content in primary school mathematics, however. There is indeed a substantial area of common ground which will figure in the mathematics teaching of most primary schools. What will vary will be the emphasis placed on different elements of the syllabus.

An attempt will be made here, by drawing on recent influential publications, to outline those aspects of mathematics which are likely to feature in some form in the majority of primary school syllabuses, even though balance and priority will vary from school to school. As this analysis proceeds, two critical questions of balance and relevance will emerge in relation to the commercial scheme. First of all, how far does the scheme reflect the balance of importance which a particular school might accord to the various elements of a mathematics programme and secondly, what kind of contribution might a scheme realistically make in relation to each of these elements?

Aims

Each school will have certain aims in mind when teaching mathematics and these are likely to be specified in any curriculum document which has been devised within the school. These aims may be the result of consultation among staff or they may be laid down by the headteacher; they may be expressed in very general terms or they may be set out in some detail. However they have been arrived at and whatever final form they take, it is likely that certain fundamental issues will have been considered. The HMI document, *Mathematics from 5–11* (1979), suggests what these might be:

The general *aims* should be to develop:

i   a positive attitude to mathematics as an interesting and attractive subject;

ii an appreciation of the creative aspects of the subject and an awareness of its aesthetic appeal;

iii an ability to think clearly and logically in mathematics and with confidence, independence of thought and flexibility of mind;

iv an understanding of mathematics through a process of enquiry and experiment;

v   an appreciation of the nature of numbers and of space, leading to an awareness of the basic structure of mathematics;

vi an appreciation of mathematical pattern and the ability to identify relationships;

vii mathematical skills and knowledge accompanied by the quick recall of basic facts;

viii an awareness of the uses of mathematics in the world beyond the classroom. Children should learn that mathematics will frequently help them to solve problems they meet in everyday life or understand better many of the things they see, and provide opportunities for them to satisfy their curiosity and to use their creative abilities;

ix persistence through sustained work in mathematics which requires some perseverance over a period of time. (p. 5)

The emphasis given to these issues may vary widely from school to school. Some, for example, may consider the ability to think mathematically to be of great importance while others may consider the present needs of the child to understand his everyday world to be the matter of prime concern. Some may regard mathematical skills and knowledge as their immediate goal while others may be more preoccupied with promoting an enjoyment of the subject. It is not that one aim is likely to exclude another but rather it is a matter of where priorities are placed.

Whatever pattern of aims is agreed for mathematics, it is important that they should be consistent with the general aims of the school. If the general aims focus on the acquisition of basic skills, for example, then a curriculum aim to promote mathematical understanding through exploration and discovery might, however desirable, unfortunately prove unrealistic in practice. This does not simply indicate that aims in mathematics should be made to fit in with those of the school. It may well be that an examination of aims in mathematics could lead to the reverse operation; aims in the school could be brought more into line with those in mathematics. The point is consistency rather than domination.

Many schemes set out their aims clearly at the beginning, or in the teacher's handbook, and this offers some indication of the degree of consistency that might be expected. This is not of itself sufficient guidance, however, for the materials may not on closer inspection appear to fulfil the stated aims. In particular, the balance of importance implied in the statement may not be maintained. A more thorough examination will be needed to establish which are the principal aims the materials are constructed to fulfil. A scheme may claim to encourage positive attitudes and appreciation of the creative and aesthetic aspects of mathematics, for example, but if the subject matter is dull it may be only the virtue of persistence that it fosters.

Content

Bell, Costello and Küchemann (1983) conclude from a review of research on the teaching of mathematics that there is general agreement that mathematical understanding rests upon three distinct forms of knowledge: skills, conceptual structures and general strategies. Conceptual structures are 'richly interconnected bodies of knowledge', which depend on an appreciation of how a piece of mathematical learning relates to what is already known and understood. Skills consist of discrete facts and routine procedures such as those involved in computation. General strategies involve the ability to approach a problem with confidence that it is capable of mathematical solution and to select appropriate skills and knowledge for this purpose. Such an ability includes an appreciation of the nature of mathematics and of what it can achieve.

It is not difficult to find descriptions of the topics which are generally considered to be appropriate areas for primary school children to study in order to build up mathematical understanding. Two HMI discussion documents, *A View of the Curriculum* (1980) and *Mathematics from 5–11* (1979) give such outlines.

The danger in drawing up lists of topics to be dealt with, however, is that it may appear that once something has been covered it can be crossed off the list. It is important that the approach should rather be one of constant spiralling return so that knowledge is renewed and applied to different situations and networks of understanding are extended. Thus the concept of 'same shape' acquired in relation to all squares regardless of size might at first sight be applied to rectangles until closer inspection forces a refinement and hence an extension of the conceptual structure.

Bell, Costello and Küchemann find that the kind of knowledge that children build up in mathematics depends very much on the relative attention given by the teacher to skills, conceptual structures and general strategies. If a teacher concentrates most effort on distinct basic skills, for example, children may have difficulty either in relating those skills conceptually to each other or in applying them strategically to real situations where they might be useful.

Similarly, the provision made in commercial schemes for the development of these forms of knowledge must be assumed to affect the pattern of children's learning. Some teachers may wish to seek a scheme which reflects the priorities which govern their own teaching. Other teachers may deliberately seek a scheme based on a different order of priorities, however, since what they require of a scheme may be something to supplement what they consider to be the least satisfactory parts of their own teaching.

Methods

As the HMI document *Mathematics from 5–11* showed, it is very difficult to consider aims without some consideration of methods. Indeed some aims in mathematics carry with them an implication of method to be employed as where an understanding of mathematics is to be developed 'through a process of enquiry and experiment'.

Once aims are agreed, therefore, certain features of method are likely to follow logically from the agreement and just as schools will vary in the emphases they give to different aims, so they will vary in the emphasis they give to different methods. In spite of this variety, however, there are certain fundamental types of teaching and learning which all schools will consider when they are attempting to establish a pattern for mathematics. The Cockcroft Report goes so far as to suggest that there are certain elements which should be considered essential in mathematics teaching at all levels. These are:

exposition by the teacher;

discussion between teacher and pupils and between pupils themselves;

appropriate practical work;

consolidation and practice of fundamental skills and routines;

problem solving, including the application of maths to everyday situations;

investigational work. (§ 243)

Many primary classrooms will include all of these elements but the frequency with which they occur will vary greatly. Many commercial schemes also imply the use of all these elements but vary in the emphasis placed upon them and therefore the assumed frequency of occurrence. If it is planned that the scheme should serve as a backbone for mathematics activities in the classroom, then it is important for the teacher to decide on the balance he or she requires and to select a scheme accordingly. Once a scheme is in use, it is inevitable that it will influence the frequency with which activities occur and this makes it all the more important for a scheme to be selected which conforms to the balance which the teacher thinks appropriate rather than the reverse. If the teacher wishes to place great emphasis, for example, on practical work and this plays only a minor role in the structure of the scheme under consideration, then that scheme would clearly be a poor choice.

Each of the elements of mathematics teaching suggested as essential in the Cockcroft Report poses particular problems for the teacher. The kind of contribution a scheme may be able to make is likely to vary from one element to another and may be more critical in some situations than others.

'Exposition by the teacher' is perhaps the most traditional element of classroom teaching and likely to be present at some time in all primary classrooms. As the term is used here, it includes the brief questions and answers by means of which the teacher checks children's understanding and, in the case of the skilful teacher, extends it. It is clear, from a later discussion in the Report (p. 91) that the

Committee do not see the use of schemes as eliminating the necessity for this element of teaching for they consider that most children find it very difficult to learn mathematics from the printed page. The ground needs prior preparation. Exposition is likely to remain a feature of teaching whatever scheme may be adopted, therefore, and for some teachers specific guidance on how to introduce a topic may be an important aspect of a scheme.

'Discussion' may be the most difficult element for the insecure teacher to handle and yet it is seen by the Committee as one of the most potent learning experiences for mathematics. In discussion, children reveal their confusions and misconceptions and come to terms with new concepts. Through discussion, they can arrive at an understanding of relationships and form hypotheses which may push forward that understanding. Discussion helps to bridge the gap between mathematical language and everyday situations. Through discussion children learn to become comfortable with mathematical language and hence more confident about using it.

Discussion, then, is a distinct and vital element of a mathematics programme but it occurs in conjunction with other elements. There must be a subject for discussion. The Committee show it to be an essential accompaniment to practical work, problem solving and investigational work.

The problem which discussion may pose for the teacher is that it is by its very nature unpredictable and therefore difficult to prepare for. If the teacher is unsure of how a new piece of learning relates to existing knowledge or of where it may lead, then s/he may find her/himself unable to give adequate explanations and is unlikely to be able to draw understanding out of the children or push the discussion in profitable directions. The extent to which a scheme clearly identifies the concepts underlying each topic and relates these to other concepts and groups of concepts therefore becomes crucial. Charts, diagrams, tables of contents and cross-referencing systems are all important in this respect. A

scheme which outlines points for discussion may be particularly helpful.

'Practical work' is seen as essential to the development of mathematical understanding throughout the primary years. The Cockcroft Committee do not underestimate the difficulty of organising effective practical work but see it as a necessary experience for most children. Practical activity provides them with a situation in which to think out the mathematical implications for their actions and this kind of concrete experience serves as a sound basis for the child to progress to dealing with two-dimensional representations of objects and finally to abstract ideas. The principles of secondary school geometry are likely to remain baffling to the child who has had little practical experience of shape and space.

Practical mathematical experience is recommended not only in relation to everyday situations like shopping and travel planning but also in the form of measurement, construction and manipulation of shapes in space, graphical representation of information, logical sorting of objects according to attributes and the use of structured apparatus to develop number concepts.

But practical work can be very demanding for the teacher to organise and it may not be easy to plan for the kind of progression envisaged in the Cockcroft Report. Some teachers may therefore particularly welcome a scheme which offers comprehensive suggestions for this area of mathematical experience. On the other hand, it is important for teachers to consider how realistic the demands of the practical work envisaged in a scheme may be. The space and scale of movement required must be related to the physical resources and regime of the classroom into which it might be adopted.

A further significant consideration is the flexibility of the scheme. Children vary enormously in the speed with which they are able to generalise from their experience. Practical work is very time-consuming and it is as important for them not to have too much of it as it is for them to have enough. A scheme which takes account of this and allows for flexibility in the amount of practical work that each child undertakes, has much to recommend it.

'Practice and consolidation' ensure that mathematical skills and routines are firmly established and hence easily available when children need them to solve a problem or carry out an investigation. These are perhaps the easiest activities for the teacher to organise

and the contribution that a scheme can make is in the provision of an ample supply of well ordered practice material. Again, flexibility is important for children vary in the amount of practice and consolidation they need.

'Problem solving' involves relating concepts and applying skills to particular situations. It is of major importance since it gives purpose to many of the other activities in a mathematics curriculum and can be a source of intrigue and motivation for many children. For some it presents difficulties, however, since they do not easily see which concepts and skills apply to a given problem. The extent to which a scheme promotes in children an awareness of how the concepts and skills they learn apply to real situations is therefore of considerable importance. The actual form in which problems are presented may be critical here for this may either lead children's thinking towards a solution or render the solution obscure. A scheme which is explicit about the way the

various elements within it relate to each other may also be helpful in that it enables the child as well as the teacher to build up a cognitive map of inter-relationships on which to draw in a problem situation.

'Investigational work' may arise incidentally from other work when unexpected questions are raised or it may involve the fun of mathematical tricks and puzzles. It may also be planned so that children set off on a trail of investigation which involves them in quite extensive collection and processing of data. Its importance in the mathematics curriculum is that it not only requires children to apply principles learned elsewhere but may also lead to the establishment of new ones. For the teacher one of the difficulties in devising both problem-solving and investigational work is that of sustaining ingenuity. Here an inventive and imaginative scheme can provide opportunities to supplement the ideas of the teacher.

The Cockcroft Committee were concerned to find a decline in the practice of mental mathematics in both primary and secondary classrooms. They account for this by drawing attention to the increasing use of individualised learning programmes where children work at their own pace through prepared materials and to teachers' reluctance to expose the weaknesses of the less able as was so frequently the case in 'mental arithmetic' sessions. Nevertheless, they are anxious that the decline should be reversed so that children become proficient at working things out in their head, forming rough estimates, explaining how they arrived at answers and so on. This kind of mental work, free from the laboriousness of written recording, is seen as essential in promoting speed and confidence and in developing insights which can support work in establishing skills and routines, problem solving and investigation.

It may be that most teachers look not to a mainstream scheme but to purpose-built supplementary materials for help in providing for mental mathematics. Nevertheless, the position which a scheme designed to be comprehensive adopts on this issue may affect the confidence which teachers place in it.

Assessment

Assessment performs a vital function in all areas of the curriculum but its role can seldom be discerned as clearly as in mathematics. It can inform both teacher and child about collective and individual progress; it can help a teacher to diagnose the difficulties of an individual child and it can provide a basis for planning future learning activities both for the individual and for the group as a whole. Which of these functions predominates depends on the priorities of the school. Some schools may emphasise the first: the traditional Friday morning arithmetic test, for example, remains a feature of school life for many primary children. In others more weight is given to the prescriptive aspect of assessment: a knowledge of present performance can ensure that all forms of mathematical experience provided are appropriate to children's current level of functioning.

Assessment may be by means of standardised tests if the aim is to relate a given child or group of children to children in general, but if the aim is to find out what they are good at so as to illuminate future planning then criterion-referenced tests may be more suitable. These focus on particular skills and can often be made up by the teacher without outside assistance.

The most common way of assessing mathematics is by means of a written test, but while such tests are simple to administer they may not enable children to demonstrate the true level of their mathematical understanding. Oral testing and practical testing of the type pioneered by the APU offer some children a better opportunity to show what they are capable of.

It is essential that whatever form of assessment is used, it should be appropriate to what is assumed to have been learned and to the use to which it is to be put. Undoubtedly, some aspects of mathematics are more easily assessed than others: 'fundamental skills and routines', for example, lend themselves to simple forms of testing where the quality of 'investigational work' is much more difficult to

11

determine. Consequently, there is always a danger that some areas of experience may be over-assessed and some relatively neglected in this respect. It is also true that some uses of assessment make more demands on the teacher than others. Communicating class positions to children is much easier than planning programmes on the basis of lessons drawn from assessment, and there may be some temptation to neglect assessment-based planning; indeed Eggleston (1983) felt that so little educational use had been made of the massive APU testing programme in mathematics that he felt constrained to draw out some of the implications himself.

Some tasks associated with assessment in mathematics, then, are difficult and require considerable professional ingenuity. Nevertheless, an assessment policy should reflect the real, stated priorities, the aims and the preferred ways of learning in the school rather than be governed by what is easiest and least demanding. This is as true for work associated with a scheme as it is for any other part of the mathematics programme. Assessment is an integral part of many mathematics schemes; it may be that this is simply a matter of suggestions or it may be that a particular system is prescribed and the materials for assessment are included. Whichever is the case, the assessment procedures must be compatible with the aims and objectives of the scheme which in turn, of course, should be compatible with those of the school. Like assessment in other areas of mathematical activity, the procedures associated with a scheme should be sufficiently comprehensive to sample all aspects of the work involved and sufficiently flexible to allow for the variety of ways in which a teacher might wish to use them, whether for monitoring, diagnosis or forward planning.

Where a scheme provides its own in-built assessment procedures, it is important that they should be readily comprehensible by both children and teacher. It should be clear, for example, whether the findings are meant to relate to other children in the country or simply to particular skills or areas covered by the scheme. It should also be possible for children to see the progress they have made and to gain an idea of the things they are good at and the areas where more work is needed.

The use of a scheme can provide the basis for a systematic approach to the general assessment of mathematics in the classroom but there are dangers. A scheme can offer one of the simplest and most immediate forms of feedback for children; this in itself makes it essential that the feedback is fair and comprehensive and not confined to a particular aspect of mathematics or a particular type of performance. A scheme can also provide the teacher with invaluable information to help in selecting further appropriate activities, but this makes it all the more important for this kind of selection to be feasible. This requires that the scheme can be used with flexibility and that children are not locked into an unvarying channel.

The usefulness of any form of assessment is in part dependent on the way in which results are recorded. Clear records of performance must be kept if assessment is to do anything other than provide information of interest at the time but soon forgotten. On the other hand, selectivity is crucial. Unless teachers are to spend the major part of their professional life on records, only the most telling aspects of performance can be noted. For many teachers, setting up a satisfactory system of record keeping is a major problem.

A mathematics scheme may be a help here. It may suggest or provide a system which at the least keeps that area of work under control and may even form the basis of recording other areas of mathematical experience. Indeed, this may be one of the most important aspects for a teacher to examine: schemes which confine recording to performance (pages, sections completed) are likely to be both less illuminating and less adaptable than those with more generalised recording bases concerned with achievements of skill and understanding.

3 The scheme

What should a teacher look for in a commercially produced mathematics scheme? Some of the requirements arise naturally from earlier discussions. Most basic of these is that a scheme which claims to be comprehensive should cover those skills, conceptual structures and general strategies that are considered to form appropriate content for children of primary school age.

A comprehensive scheme should also make provision for a full range of teaching and learning activities such as that specified in the Cockcroft Report (1982) so that teachers can find guidance on setting up all kinds of learning situations and children can be involved in a variety of ways of working.

Other requirements concern the way that the scheme is organised and presented, the form in which it is produced and the demands it makes on the teacher and the learning situation. A thorough investigation of these aspects of a scheme is necessary before any sensible judgement about its suitability can be made.

Organisation

Above all, a scheme needs to be organised logically so that novel concepts rest on existing understanding and children are not put in a position of trying to master new material on the basis of incomplete understanding of essential earlier work. As Eggleston (1983) shows in his analysis of the six APU Reports on mathematics so far produced, insufficient prior understanding is one of the most common causes of failure.

However logically a scheme is organised it will be difficult to operate unless the organisational basis is specified so that those who use it, both teachers and children, understand the pattern. Not only does it need to be evident precisely what teacher and children are ex-

pected to be doing but also why they are doing it and how it relates to other things that they have done. Visual presentation in such forms as charts and diagrams is one of the ways in which sequencing and assumptions may be clarified.

Practical advice may also be necessary to help teachers to operate the scheme. They may find it useful to be informed about the way children are expected to tackle a piece of work and the method of calculation they are supposed to be using. Where a priority in a scheme is claimed to be establishing links with other areas of the curriculum it is reasonable to expect specific suggestions as to how this can be achieved.

Flexibility is also an important attribute. A scheme which allows children to begin at whatever level is appropriate to their achievement and to receive more or less practice at any particular point according to their individual needs has clear advantages in a mixed ability situation and when children transfer from another school. Similarly, while it is essential for the coherence of a scheme that all the parts fit logically together, it may be important for some teachers to be able to use the parts separately when the occasion demands.

Presentation

The presentation of the scheme has a considerable effect on the attitudes of those who use it. In part, this is a question of the visual impact which the scheme makes, its attractiveness, whether it is colourful and relevantly illustrated with a print layout which is conducive to understanding rather than confusion. In part also, it is a question of the situations and activities which are used as a vehicle for the mathematics: contemporary settings which are meaningful to children and activities which they enjoy are most likely to promote positive attitudes.

Perhaps most important of all, however, is that the requirements of the scheme should be formulated in such a way that children are able to cope with them. The text should be written in language which can be read and understood by the children for whom it is intended. This aspect requires particular scrutiny on the part of the teacher for, as studies attempting to apply readability formulae to mathematics texts have shown (see, for example, Lunzer and Gardner, 1979), deceptively simple language can conceal ideas which are conceptually very difficult. Care should be taken with syntax and the use of symbols. New vocabulary, particularly anything of a technical nature, should be introduced in a way and at a pace which makes it capable of assimilation. Graphs, charts and diagrams should be clear, and easy to interpret; lay-out should be simple to follow. As Shuard and Rothery (1984) show, for some children, forms of verbal and visual presentation which should clarify mathematics can all too easily lead to greater confusion.

Problems should be presented in a clear style and with a full awareness of the difference that visual, spatial and concrete aids and simple non-technical language make to children's capacity to perform mathematical tasks. The aim throughout should be to make thorough provision for experiences which are motivating and which extended children's abilities without adding to the anxiety with which many of them approach mathematics.

Format

Schemes are produced in a variety of forms and listing the actual components is perhaps the easiest part of any analysis. It can soon be established what the scheme consists of in terms of children's materials, such as work books/sheets/cards, spirit masters, text books and so on. It is also a simple task to list the materials for teachers and additional features such as tapes and computer programs. Questions will remain about the quality of the components, however.

Materials that children will use must be serviceable, strong enough to withstand the rigours of classroom use and protected wherever possible so that they do not become dirty too quickly. In most classrooms, space is always insufficient and all parts of a scheme should be as compact as is consistent with use by children. There should also be an efficient storage system so that materials can be taken out and put away with as little disruption as possible.

Choosing a scheme involves the school in a large financial investment. Initial cost is important but this has to be viewed against the extensiveness of coverage provided by the scheme and the degree to which materials are consumable and will therefore need replacing. Factors such as these determine the value for money offered by the scheme, which for all primary schools is a central consideration.

Finally, the teacher's materials should be laid out with equal clarity. They should specify for whom the scheme is suitable and how it should be used. Ideally, they should provide all the key information the teacher is likely to need in order to be able to operate the scheme and they should dovetail at every stage with the children's work.

Demands

The demands which a scheme makes on a teacher and a classroom can be a critical factor in determining whether it is suitable for adoption. If it requires facilities which the school cannot supply then it will not be used as intended and is therefore unlikely to prove a sound choice.

An assessment needs to be made, therefore, of what will be required in the way of apparatus, materials and resources such as calculators and computers. A school which does not possess them needs to discover how easily available these are. Similarly there needs to be a realistic comparison of the space required for the activities envisaged with the space actually available in the classroom. Where the teacher is expected to create working materials to supplement the scheme, it is important to discover how much help is given to guide the teacher in this task. Assessments such as these will be made more easily with some schemes than others, for schemes vary not only in the demands they make but also in the degree of clarity with which they specify what will be needed and the advice they offer on how to obtain or create anything that may be lacking.

4 The people

The successful use of a mathematics scheme essentially requires a sympathetic match between the people who create it and those who use it. If the aspirations of one are out of line with the beliefs and capabilities of the other, the materials are unlikely to be used successfully. To ensure a good match, two kinds of investigation are necessary. First, as much as possible needs to be known about the people involved in the creation of the scheme and the circumstances of its development. Secondly, an honest appraisal needs to be made by the users of the scheme not only of themselves but also of their situation and the children for whom they are responsible. The degree of congruence between the creators and the users can then be assessed.

Authors

Most schemes do indicate the names of the authors, but they do not always supply the kind of information a teacher would like to know. Teachers are bound to be interested in the professional experience of the authors, how much time they have actually spent teaching in classrooms and whether they have been in a position to understand not only their own teaching problems but those of others. In addition, it is helpful to know what the authors believe about the purpose of mathematics teaching and its place in the primary school curriculum.

Finding out about the authors themselves usually brings with it information about the way in which the scheme came into being. A scheme produced co-operatively as part of an in-service activity by a working party of teachers, for instance, is likely to be quite different in nature from one created by a writer working alone. A scheme designed in another country is also likely to have distinctive qualities about it. This does not mean that

one form of origin will necessarily lead to superior materials; there are likely to be different advantages and handicaps associated with different forms of creation. But a prospective user who knows how a scheme came into being will have some idea of its likely strengths.

If field trials of the materials have taken place, they will have influenced the final form and here it is useful to know at what stage of production the trials took place and what kind of children were involved in the procedure. A good match may well result if the children were of similar age, ability level and social background to those for whom a scheme is required. Information about the way a scheme comes into being can have a considerable effect on the confidence with which a decision to adopt can be made.

Teachers

While it is the classroom teacher who will have day-to-day responsibility for operating a mathematics scheme, the decision to choose a particular scheme is more likely to be a school-wide rather than an individual decision. The scheme must suit the school as a whole and its ways of working and, in some cases, it may be necessary to satisfy requirements which extend beyond the institution itself. The LEA, for instance, may have a policy or guidelines for mathematics which will affect the decision.

Nevertheless, the success or failure of the scheme in practice will depend very largely on the teachers who will be working with it so it is important that they should feel comfortable with the scheme. It has already been suggested that teachers need to be clear in their own mind about their aims in teaching mathematics, the approaches they intend to adopt and the working systems they would like to put into operation. This will help to clarify the reasons for using a scheme and how it is to be used, whether as an overall framework for teaching or simply as a means of supplementing it where the need is felt to be greatest.

Teachers also need to be honest and rigorous in their appraisal of themselves, their priorities and their personal strengths and weaknesses. They must examine their own beliefs about mathematics, how high a priority they are prepared to give to it and how they think it relates to other areas of the curriculum. They must be honest about such matters as whether they enjoy the subject, whether they feel confident in teaching it and whether they have sufficient knowledge and experience to create their own structures and to teach it well. Their answers to these questions will help them decide on the level and detail of explanation necessary in the scheme they might choose, the extent of the guidance offered and possibly the availability of training sessions in the use of it. A scheme which seems condescending and dictatorial to one teacher may offer a lifeline to another.

Children

Just as important as finding a scheme which the teacher can work with is finding one which the children will enjoy and be able to cope with. Every group of children, composed as it is of individuals, is distinct and different from every other. The first stage in buying an 'off the peg' mathematics scheme must be to examine the group for whom it is intended for only in this way can a teacher be sure of getting the best possible 'fit'.

On whatever basis the group has been formed, it is likely to contain children of varying mathematical ability, but the range of variation may differ. The scheme required by a broadly homogeneous group of children will be different in structure from one which will be useful with a group of varied ability. The level of ability must also be taken into account. A group containing children of very low ability will need a scheme adequately supplied with activities concerned with concrete situations while a group containing gifted children will need materials which offer sufficient opportunities for extension through investigational work.

Whatever their ability, children learn in different ways. Some, for example, may work best by building up a gradual picture from small items of learning while others work best if they get an idea of the total picture first and then have the opportunity to break this down into constituent parts. Ready-made schemes are unlikely to offer both approaches to the same content but it may be important either that different approaches are offered in the course of the scheme or that approaches are capable of modification where necessary.

Like teachers, children vary considerably in their attitudes. Mathematics is a difficult subject which arouses anxiety in many learners. This has been found to be particularly so with girls who are apt to reject the subject as being beyond their capabilities. The more children there are with feelings of inadequacy and anxiety the more important it may be to find a scheme with clear explanations and a gradient of difficulty which does not increase too sharply. Even where the children do not lack confidence, they may easily be alienated by material and activities that are difficult, dull or unrelated to their real life. In particular, children from minority racial groups or children from exclusive social settings such as inner city or rural areas may find little to relate to in a scheme which draws its situations from a fictitious, bland or universalised life style. Factors such as these may have a considerable influence not only on children's motivation but also on their ability to understand.

In the final analysis, it is children's understanding and enjoyment which are the most important considerations of all. If the materials do not make it easier for children to develop insights and see connections not only within mathematics but also between mathematics and their everyday lives, if they do not promote enjoyment and appreciation of mathematics, then they have failed to perform their chief function.

A scheme may appear excellent on paper but whether it will work in a given situation is very largely a matter of whether those who use it take to it. Taste is always unpredictable. It is difficult to be completely sure that those who work with a scheme will find that it fulfils their needs but it is possible to reduce the risk by the kind of thorough personal analysis suggested here. The next step is to undertake an analysis of the schemes on offer so those which do not match the established requirements can be eliminated. Such an analysis needs to be conducted systematically, taking full account of those issues relating to the teaching of mathematics to primary school children which have been discussed in this chapter. A schedule of criteria which could be used for this purpose follows and the schedule is then illustratively applied to a variety of major schemes currently available.

PART TWO

A Schedule of Suggested Criteria for Examining Mathematics Schemes

1 *Characteristics, design and construction*

Publication

1 What was the date of first publication?
2 Is this a revised edition? If so, when was it revised?
3 Is it a complete primary scheme or a supplementary scheme?
4 If it is a supplementary scheme what contribution is it expected to make?
5 Under whose influence, patronage or funding was the series produced – commercial publisher, a college or university mathematics centre, a local education authority, The Schools Council, an educational foundation?
6 Does the publisher have a good reputation and possess significant experience of publishing texts and materials for the primary schools sector?
7 Were the materials field tested before publication? Where? When? How?
8 What is the country of origin of the scheme?

Authorship

1 What are the names of the authors?
2 What are the qualifications and professional backgrounds of the authors? In particular, have they had recent practical experience of teaching mathematics to the target age group?

Design, Production and Provision

1 What general materials are available for use by children? Are they text books? Work books? Ready-printed work sheets? Spirit duplicator masters? Work cards?
2 What general materials are available for use by teachers? Is there a resource book? Notes? Answer books?
3 What additional materials are provided? Transparencies? Audio tapes? Videotapes? Computer software?
4 If these are not provided are items recommended and ideas offered?
5 Is essential equipment provided or recommended? Is the 'hardware' capable of improvised production by the child or teacher?
6 Are additional specific resources required, such as calculators?
7 Are the materials consumable?
8 Are the materials easily available in sufficient quantities?
9 Are the infant and junior stage materials separately designed and organised? Are they fully compatible?
10 Can the scheme be divided into sections to allow distribution throughout a school to cater for special needs of groups and individuals, and the particular organisational structure of the school?
11 Are the books strongly bound and capable of staying open at a page without damage to the binding?
12 Are the work cards laminated? Are storage boxes and/or envelopes provided? Are they robust enough and do they allow versatility of use without damage?
13 Are the books and games compact enough to be used on an average school desk?
14 Are the materials for children easy to handle, store, distribute and collect?
15 Are the materials generally attractive and

colourful, making good use of photographs, diagrams, pictures and colour? Do the illustrations contribute to the usefulness of the scheme?

16 Is the general style of presentation up to date and interesting?

Cost

1 What would be the basic cost of introducing the scheme into a school
(*a*) In the first year?
(*b*) In subsequent years?

2 Aims, objectives and scope of the scheme

Aims and Objectives

1 Are the general aims of the scheme clearly specified?
2 If not, is it possible to determine the general aims?
3 Is any weighting attached to the aims?
4 Are the specific objectives within the scheme consistent with the general aims?
5 Are the objectives of particular sections specified in such a way that we can assess whether they have been achieved?
6 Do the aims and objectives imply the predominant use of a particular approach or method for teaching and learning? In particular, is the emphasis on teacher direction or child self-direction?

General Content, Approach and Activities

1 Are the mathematical concepts, skills and generalisations to be developed clearly identified for each topic, section and page?
2 Are the suggested activities consistent with the stated aims and specific objectives?
3 Do the materials and methods require special facilities with regard to use of space and grouping of children?
4 Are clear reasons given for carrying out the activities specified for the various topics?
5 Does the scheme encourage use and facility with different materials, kinds of structural apparatus and approaches?
6 Do the objectives and activities specify the range of equipment and methods of calculation to be used?

Scope

1 Does the scheme specify the type of learners for which it has been designed in terms of age, range of ability and sex?
2 Does the scheme provide outlines of the structure and inter-relationships of the content in flow diagrams, matrix charts, a cross-referenced index, concept groupings? Are they easy to understand and illuminating for the teacher?
3 Do the suggested activities include opportunities (as suggested by the Cockcroft Report) for: exposition by the teacher; discussion between teacher and pupils and between pupils themselves; appropriate practical work; consolidation and practice of fundamental skills and routines; problem solving, including the application of mathematics to everyday situations; investigational work?
4 Do the situations and examples refer to up-to-date circumstances at home and in society?
5 Does the content support the suggested approach and methods of teaching?
6 What is the emphasis on different forms of knowledge such as skills; conceptual structures; general strategies?
7 What priority is attached to each aspect of the mathematics curriculum at each specified level? Are any aspects neglected and at which level?
8 Are the materials capable of being used in other curricular areas such as science, geography and craft?

Sequence

1 Is the approach 'spiral', returning continually to previous situations and problems to re-examine them in the light of extended knowledge?
2 Is the sequencing designed to show the interrelationships within mathematics or to concentrate on reinforcement of learning?
3 Is the presentation of ideas in the children's materials clear and logical?
4 Are facilities provided for integrating children who transfer from other schools? Is the sequencing flexible enough to allow the scheme to be used from a mid-point?

3 The scheme in relation to teachers

1 What materials are available or required for use by teachers, for example, teachers' books, special visual aids, etc?
2 Is the teacher's book comprehensive, easy to read and easy to use to relate teaching to the children's activities?
3 Is it strongly bound and free from errors?
4 Does it provide evidence to substantiate its suggested approach?
5 Does it provide clear instructions about ways to teach the topic?
6 Does it provide clear information about essential materials and equipment required to teach specific topics?
7 Does it provide information for the teacher about the mathematics underlying the children's activities?
8 Does it encourage or allow the use of various types of classroom organisation and grouping?
9 Does it offer advice with regard to supervision and safety when children are carrying out practical activities?
10 Are the aims and objectives written in such a way as to be meaningful to teachers

– would colleagues understand what each other had been teaching and why?
11 Are provisions made for modification by the teacher of the scope, sequence and pace of work to meet the needs of individual differences, for example in learning styles, sex, intelligence, linguistic competence and motivation?
12 Would the scheme encourage teacher enjoyment of mathematics?
13 Does the scheme make particular demands on a teacher's classroom management skills, for example grouping children, child involvement, marking, production and selection of additional materials?
14 How realistic are the demands on a teacher's time of the various organisational/educational requirements of the scheme?
15 Is a teacher training facility provided or available to ensure proper use of the materials?
16 Are facilities provided for the education of parents with regard to the content and approach used in the scheme?

4 The scheme in relation to children

1 Is there a social or cultural bias in the choice of examples or in the design of the teaching/learning sections?
2 Are special materials provided or recommended for special groups of learners, for example children with learning difficulties or particular handicaps such as colour blindness or dyslexia?
3 Are facilities provided for individualising a child's learning in mathematics?
4 Are the objectives clearly specified and meaningful to children? Could a child explain to a teacher or another child why he or she has been carrying out a particular activity?
5 Do the design, style and expected activities appear likely to interest children? Would the use of the scheme be likely to encourage enjoyment of mathematics?
6 Would the use of the scheme be likely to foster anxiety in children?
7 Does the scheme seem likely to require substantial interest, perseverance and general self-motivation by children?
8 Are the practice exercises likely to be motivational for children, for example, 'Can you do these?', 'How many can you do in one minute?'
9 Are clear instructions given to children about amounts of peer group co-operation available or required in the activities and exercises?

5 Language

1 Do the materials require a level of reading ability appropriate to the age and ability of the target group of children, particularly in terms of decoding words, coping with sentence and paragraph length, understanding the vocabulary and relating to the subject matter?

2 Is adequate provision made for the introduction of technical vocabulary, particularly words peculiar to mathematics (for example, hypotenuse); words with special mathematical meanings (for example, odd) and words with dual mathematical meanings (for example, base)?

3 How effectively are ideas and instructions communicated with regard to clarity of language, use of diagrams, subheadings, etc., and use of symbols, signals, prompts, etc?

4 Is the size of print appropriate to the target group of children?

5 Is the layout clear and likely to promote comprehension?

6 Does the scheme encourage discussion?

7 Is the scheme likely to promote the ability to talk confidently about mathematical ideas?

6 Assessment and record keeping

1 Are tests and other instruments of assessment of the child's progress provided? If not, are suitable items recommended?
2 Do the provided or recommended items supply immediate feedback for teachers and for children?
3 Is continuous assessment an integral part of the scheme so that success or failure can be diagnosed early and easily, and treated immediately?
4 Are expected minimum levels of achievement and competency specified to encourage more able children to accelerate and enrich the pace and scope of learning?
5 Are the provided or recommended assessment materials criterion-referenced or norm-referenced?
6 Do the provided or recommended assessment materials allow profiling of a child's experience and ability in the various aspects of mathematics?
7 Are the provided or recommended assessment procedures compatible with the priorities of the scheme?
8 Is guidance given to teachers to develop and construct their own assessment materials?
9 Are facilities provided or suggested for accurate record keeping by teachers and children?
10 Do the suggested modes of record keeping list cards/pages completed or the achievement of specified objectives?

7 Supplementary questions for the individual teacher and school

1 Are the aims of the scheme in agreement with and suitable for the school, community and local education authority in which you work?

2 Are the structure, scope and approach of the scheme in accord with the mathematics curriculum of feeder and subsequent schools?

3 Do you agree with the emphasis of the scheme in terms of content and required teaching methods?

4 Do you agree with the emphasis of the scheme in terms of the required practical work and child involvement?

5 Is the scheme in accord with the existing approach used in the school and with likely future developments?

6 Is the attitude to mathematics encouraged by use of the scheme in accord with the general attitudes of staff and children?

7 Does the target user group of the scheme match that of your school in terms of age, ability, social background?

8 Does the suggested style of working in the scheme fit in with the school's ways of working in other curricular areas?

9 What new content would have to be mastered by the teachers in the school before the scheme could become fully operational?

10 Can your school afford to set up the scheme – with the necessary equipment required in addition to the books and other materials – in the short term? What would the long-term expense require in terms of transfer of resources from other curricular areas?

PART THREE

Applying the Criteria to Currently Available Mathematics Schemes

1 Characteristics, design and construction

Date of publication and revisions

A large number of the mathematics schemes currently on the market are very recent publications. Many, including *Ginn Mathematics*, *Step by Step Mathematics* (Blackie), *Peak Mathematics* (Nelson), *IMP* (Cambridge), *Mastermaths* (Oxford), *Macmillan Junior Maths*, and *Racing to Maths* (Hulton), are products of the 1980s. For several of these the situation is by no means static since plans to continue to add to the scheme or provide additional related material appear likely to carry on through most of the decade. This is the case for *Peak*, *Ginn*, and *Step by Step*, for example. Such plans enable publishers to respond to developments such as the increasing availability of microcomputers in primary schools and tailor their materials accordingly.

In view of this level of activity in mathematics publishing, no school looking for a scheme needs to consider materials prepared for a different generation of children or written without the benefits of recent developments in research and thinking about mathematics teaching. Recency of publication does not, of course, guarantee suitability or an enlightened and informed approach but it does make them more likely. One possible drawback of recency is that the scheme may still be in the process of development and the purchase of a scheme on the basis of its early parts requires something of an act of faith.

Several earlier schemes including *Mathematics for Schools* ('Fletcher Maths', Addison Wesley), *SMP* (Cambridge) and *Beta Mathematics* (Schofield and Sims) have recently been revised. The extent of the revision varies greatly from the relatively superficial changes in *Beta Mathematics* to the thorough overhaul to which the early parts of *SMP* have

recently been subjected. Revision may by no means ensure improvement: the reduction of page size in *Beta* is actually unhelpful. But revision is an indication that publisher and authors are still actively thinking about and concerned for their materials. It may provide an opportunity to include more examples where experience has shown this to be necessary (as in *SMP*), or to improve sequence and presentation (*Mathematics for Schools*). It may even allow for developments which would not have been considered appropriate when the scheme was first published. The Parents' Booklet to accompany *Mathematics for Schools* is a development of this kind.

With some schemes, there seem to have been second thoughts about the provision of teachers' materials. A teacher's book has been added late in life to *Kites* (Evans) and *Beta*, while in *Peak* an extension of teachers' materials has been undertaken since main publication of the scheme. Such a development can be suspected as post-rationalisation of materials which were insufficiently thought through in the first place or it could be welcomed as evidence that the authors are constantly seeking to improve the quality of guidance offered and to respond to feedback from the classroom. Prospective users must consider which of these explanations is the more likely in the light of the philosophy expressed in the teachers' books, the extent to which the advice offered is helpful and convincing and the timing of the publication.

Intended scope of the scheme

For most schemes to which reference will be made in this section, the claim is made that they are comprehensive schemes which require little or no supplementary material. This aim of the modern scheme to be completely comprehensive leads in many cases to systems which are so complex that they appear confusing. *Ginn*, *Peak* and *Step by Step*, for instance, might present an intimidating picture at first sight, with their workbooks, work cards, assessment and recording devices, resource packs, duplicating masters and so on, and there may be some temptation to select only parts of the scheme rather than use the materials in the fully integrated way intended. On the other hand, the systems may be more easily mastered than initial impressions of complexity would suggest.

Other schemes such as *Macmillan Junior Mathematics* and *Mastermaths* may appear attractive in their simplicity. Though they claim to be comprehensive, the main books have little or nothing in the way of appendages. *Mastermaths*, for example, consists of a single pupil's book and a teacher's resource book at each of four levels. Such economy is achieved chiefly by parsimony in the advice offered to teachers and an expectation that teachers will photocopy resource and activity pages for use with children. There is a basic equation between the degree of advice and provision offered to the teacher and the degree of complexity presented by the scheme. Only the user can decide on the value to be placed on each side of the equation.

To some extent, complexity is also a product of age range. Those schemes which cater only for older children, for example *SMP*, *Mastermaths*, *Arnold Junior Maths* and *Macmillan Junior Mathematics* or only for younger children, for example *IMP*, *Kites* and *Macmillan Mathematics* can afford to be apparently less complex than those like *Peak*, *Nuffield*, *Step by Step* and *Ginn* which cater for a full primary age range.

Supplementary materials abound and are generally designed to contribute to one particular element in the teaching and learning of mathematics such as mental mathematics, for example *Five a Day* (Oliver and Boyd); computational skills, for example *Number Practice* (Schofield and Sims), or problem solving, for example, *Let's Solve Problems* (Basil Blackwell).

Since they aim to provide experience in one narrowly defined area, they generally perform this function at least adequately. The important thing for the teacher is to recognise both their limitations and their potential usefulness. Whatever the claimed breadth of a main scheme, supplementary materials may still be necessary with a teaching group which consists of children of widely differing abilities where some may need more practice and some more extension than a general scheme can provide.

Origins of the scheme

Schemes vary greatly in their origins and in the information that they supply about those origins. Similarly, teachers may vary in the importance they attach to this kind of information; some may be content to judge the product by its quality while others may feel reassured to know something of the circumstances in which it has been devised.

The authorship of courses is almost always acknowledged although there are exceptions: *Ginn* credits only its British adaptor. Few are published as the work of a single author although this is the case with *Mastermaths* by Paul Briten. More frequently, schemes depend on a partnership. *Step by Step* is written by two authors, *Peak* by three. Both *IMP* and *SMP* acknowledge a writing team.

Where a single author is involved, there may be the advantages of clarity of conception and consistency of style but the scheme may also be limited by its dependence on the ingenuity of one person and by the fact that that person is unlikely to be equally familiar with all stages of mathematics learning. Where a team of writers is used, there is scope for specialist writing for the different age groups and it may be easier for a team to generate inventive ideas. The dangers may lie in the possibilities of inconsistency among different writers and omission if each is responsible for only one section. This disadvantage is usually overcome by the appointment of a general editor who takes responsibility for co-ordinating the work and ensuring continuity. Eric Albany, for example, performs this task for *Nuffield*.

The credibility of the authors will depend on such matters as their qualifications, where they work and the experience they have, particularly of teaching children of the age range for whom the materials are intended. Interestingly, publishers only rarely give any information about the qualifications of their writers; *Step by Step* is an exception here. Their place of work is much more likely to be mentioned although whether a prospective user should be more impressed by a team made up predominantly of college lecturers and advisers as is the case with *Mathematics for Schools*, or by a team which consists exclusively of primary school headteachers (*Peak*) is difficult to decide. One group is close to the classroom while the other is in a position to gain an overall view of the things teachers find difficult and easy. Experience of teaching the relevant age group, at some time, is widely considered to be important and it is unusual to find publishers who do not emphasise this aspect of their authors' experience. *Nuffield*, *SMP*, *IMP* and *Peak*, for example, all make much of this and it is interesting to note that where a scheme like *Ginn* cannot provide this sort of information about its authors, it takes care to list a panel of teacher consultants. Schemes like *Beta* and *Kites* are exceptional in the complete absence of information about their authors and what experience they have which qualifies them to write the scheme.

It is important to remember, however, that if qualifications, position or experience were sufficient to ensure excellence in a mathematics scheme, there would be almost as many good schemes as there are teachers. Such factors can only be regarded as likely pointers to quality.

Schemes owe much to the circumstances of their birth and these, too, vary greatly. Some appear to be due to straightforward publishing initiatives: *Ginn* and *Racing to Maths* are of this type and seem to be an attempt by the publishers to repeat the success that they have experienced with schemes in the field of reading. Others are the result of substantial curriculum development projects initiated in local education authorities such as *Kent* (Ward Lock) or through bodies, agencies or foundations which regard the teaching of mathematics as their concern. Thus the Nuffield Foundation sponsored *Nuffield Mathematics* and the Scottish Education Department was responsible for setting up the original working party which led to the creation of *SPMG* (Heinemann). Such schemes tend to have been developed through considerable discussion over an extended period of time. The ideas and materials have generally been tried out with children and refined in the light of experience before publication. *Nuffield* is a particularly good example of a scheme with a long gestation period. The Nuffield Mathematics Teaching Project began in 1964 when the Nuffield Foundation sponsored teachers and mathematics specialists to look at mathematics teaching in primary schools. Guidelines for teachers were produced and many of the ideas proposed were extensively tried out and extended by teachers creating their own materials in the classroom. Only recently have the ideas been crystallised into a structured course supported by specially devised pupils' materials. The approach has benefited from years of discussion and experimentation and the materials themselves have been subjected to practical trials in schools. There has been considerable opportunity for the discovery of areas which may be weak or ill-defined, both in the approach and in the materials, and the teacher embarking on a scheme with such a developmental pedigree can at least feel confident that he or she is able to avoid mistakes that others may have made.

It would be misleading to suggest, however, that a long gestation period is a necessary prerequisite for a good scheme. An inventive writer who is also a sound mathematician may achieve in a single day what a committee may take a week to produce and the product may be just as effective.

Similarly, teachers are not always the best

guides for fellow teachers. An experienced and perceptive publisher may be better able to assess and cater for the needs of teachers than other practitioners. So although a scheme such as *Ginn* may seem rather vague as to its origins in a 'successful American programme' it may yet be able to satisfy the requirements of a primary mathematics teacher. The established reputation of a publisher can itself be an important guide.

Information about the original conception, date of publication, authorship and development of a scheme is useful. It is also important to understand its structure and complexity. Prospective users of any scheme should make it one of their first priorities to find out as much as possible about these matters and to make comparisons with the origins and scope of other schemes in which they may be interested. Such information may predispose teachers in favour of one scheme rather than another. The next step is to examine the scheme for it is the quality of the materials themselves which will provide the real basis for a choice.

Composition of materials

A most useful step in assessing materials as complex as many modern mathematics schemes tend to be is to compile a list of the component parts. This helps to sort out what children will actually be doing and what help is provided for the teacher. It also helps the prospective user to understand how the various parts of the scheme relate to each other and what is considered essential and what might be viewed as an optional extra.

Children's materials

Children's materials are chiefly of three types, namely worksheets, work cards and textbooks.

Worksheets, workbooks and spirit duplicator masters are all different means of employing the same principle, that of providing at one and the same time the stimulus for work and the space in which to respond. Work-sheets are most usually combined into work-books (for example *Mathematics for Schools*) or provided in the alternative form of spiritmasters (for example *Arnold*) which the teacher can then reproduce as required. Some schemes, such as *Nuffield* in its infant stages, provide teachers with a choice of spirit masters or worksheets.

Since worksheets are only capable of being used once, they are an expensive format for a school to adopt and the spiritmaster option, although more laborious for teachers, is one means of reducing the cost. Many schools, however, will consider the cost of the standard, one-off worksheet or workbook acceptable because there are unique advantages of the format.

First, the work can be broken down into manageable pieces so that children are not overwhelmed and can always see just where they are. Secondly, children can be provided with whatever may be the degree of support in framing their answers that the writer considers appropriate. A worksheet can require from the child a very simple response such as colouring in appropriate pictures from a display or filling in a single number in a space provided. It can also provide the framework for more complex activity such as a table in which children can report the results of practical activity, or it can require a more open-ended response such as giving a reason or an account of work carried out where nothing beyond an appropriate space is supplied. Thirdly, much of the unfruitful labour of copying out can be eliminated through the worksheet format. Sometimes, for example, worksheets are used to provide practice in computational skills where the insertion of answers is all that is required and children are spared the laborious task of writing out the sum with the scope for transcriptional errors that the process entails.

Because it is possible to devise worksheets which operate at a very simple level and give a great deal of support to the child's response, the format is used extensively with younger children. Indeed, for most schemes the work-book or worksheet is the principal vehicle for recorded work at the infant level. At junior level, worksheets are much more likely to be used as ancillary material, for 'practice' (*Nuffield*), 'reinforcement and consolidation' (*Macmillan*) or 'assessment' (*Ginn*).

If one of the key advantages of the worksheet format is accessibility for the young child, then presentation is of the utmost importance. Commonly, there is an attempt to reduce the role of language to the minimum and therefore considerable reliance on visual presentation. Unfortunately, visual perception can operate in a very idiosyncratic way and what might be clear in the first instance to the author may be open to considerable misinterpretation by the child. In *Kites* 7, page 10, for example, there is a large box of undisclosed contents with a label *10* on it and a single jar of honey beside it. To the right, a series of examples requires subtraction from 11. It is by no means clear how the 11 relates to the pictures.

It is only fair to say that it would be possible to gather examples of confusion from almost any of the schemes employing a worksheet format. It is also the case that the confusions do not come to light in many cases until children actually set out to use the materials. This is one of the reasons why materials which have been tried out in classrooms before publication have much to recommend them, although it should not be assumed that trialling necessarily results in any changes to the materials. It is also a reason why prospective users should always attempt to visit schools where a scheme is in operation before taking the major step of adopting it.

A further potential hazard of the worksheet format is that it can tempt the busy teacher into leaving children to get on by themselves since it presents a seductive image of self-sufficiency. In many cases, the reality is that the teacher may need to be on hand every step of the way. In *Mathematics for Schools*, Level 1, Book 4, page 57, for example, children are invited to halve a ball of Plasticine and then find out if the two half pieces balance each other. There are various reasons why the two half pieces of Plasticine may *not* balance each

other. The child working alone may simply write NO and a wrong concept may take shape. Again it is only fair to say that examples of this kind of difficulty can be found in most schemes.

Work cards, like worksheets, enable the writer to break the work down into pieces so that one task or cluster of tasks can be dealt with at a time. In the case of work cards, when the task has been dealt with the card can be returned and a fresh one taken. In this way, work cards create a system which children can understand and manage. The cards can be geared to any degree of difficulty required and are particularly suitable for promoting practical and investigational work since they can be carried around easily. From the teacher's point of view, they are flexible and economical in use since one card can be used successively by any number of children as they are needed for a relatively short space of time.

Work cards are particularly characteristic of junior materials where they form an important part of many schemes, for example *Ginn*, *Arnold* and *Maths Adventure*. Indeed, *SMP* relies completely on a work card system. Presumably some writers for infants fear that cards may too easily get lost and may not provide sufficient support for infants. Yet such a view does not go unchallenged for *Macmillan Mathematics* and *SPMG* make extensive use of work cards from the very beginning and *Peak* and *IMP* introduce them for older infants. So long as cards for infants are clear, well-structured and attractive, there seems no valid reason why young children should not enjoy the advantages of work card based activities.

As with worksheets, the actual presentation of the work is critical. Since the idea of a work card is that it can operate in isolation, forming a single unit of work, it is essential that all information necessary is present on the card. If it is assumed that previous cards have provided adequate preparation, then sequence becomes important and some flexibility may be sacrificed in the system.

Work cards provide varying degrees of support in structuring the answers or re-

Visual cues can be used most effectively to convey a concept. (*IMP*, Unit 2, Card 1d, Weight.)

sponses. It is important to check that sufficient support is present for the children for whom the scheme is contemplated.

There is some danger with work cards that they may lead to fragmentation in thinking and that children may not become aware of how the various tasks relate to each other mathematically. A teacher using a work card system would need to accept responsibility for establishing connections by discussing children's work with them and devoting time to sessions where links with previous work are a priority. A second danger is that a work card system may encourage an unacceptable level of trivial competition among children where completion of cards takes precedence over depth of involvement. Much depends on the climate of the classroom and the attitudes to work encouraged by the teacher.

There is one further worry on a practical level: work cards are comparatively expensive to produce but may get lost more easily than workbooks or textbooks and if too many get lost, the whole scheme may get thrown off balance. Some schemes have devised an economical answer to this problem. 'Activity card' pages are provided free of copyright, for example in *Mastermaths*, so that work cards can be easily and cheaply made and lost cards replaced by photocopying.

Textbooks provide directions for work which children then record in their own books, folders, papers or whatever classroom convention may dictate. Textbooks are usually used at junior level (for example *Ginn* and *Nuffield*) since they demand from children an ability to focus on the appropriate section of the book, to transfer their working to a different setting and to record without the benefit of external structure. Young children may find these procedures difficult and perhaps for this reason it is rare to find a textbook approach in the infant section of a scheme. It is as well to remember that for less able juniors there may well be problems too. The great advantage of textbooks, however, is that they are economical in that they are not consumed in use and may prove more durable than cards. They are also easy to store and distribute and may appear more sophisticated and therefore more acceptable to many older children.

A possible disadvantage of textbooks is that they do not offer the flexibility of worksheets or work cards in that they tend to combine into one unit a substantial allocation of work. When money has been invested in the purchase of the books and work is provided, there is some temptation to allow children simply to plough through it, whether it is appropriate or not. It would require constant planning and monitoring by teachers to ensure that individual children have enough but not too much experience of the various topics in a textbook.

Textbooks also suffer from a tendency to become deskbound. Perhaps because they are the most weighty work medium in mathematics schemes and therefore less portable than worksheets or work cards, they do appear to concern themselves frequently with activities which can be completed without the child leaving the desk. The most notable example of this tendency is *Beta Mathematics* but it is discernible in ostensibly more progressive schemes such as *Ginn* and *Arnold*.

It has been suggested that textbooks are an economical way of presenting mathematics. A note of caution is perhaps appropriate here. Some schemes such as *Nuffield* and *Step by Step* have, in the interests of economy, printed their textbooks in two colours only and these may appear dull in comparison with the full-colour printing in schemes such as *Ginn*.

Similarly, some limit the number of pages in a textbook by putting as much as possible on to each page. This may result in the somewhat crowded impression given in textbooks of certain schemes such as *Mastermaths*. If a teacher feels that the lack of colour will depress, or the crowded nature of the pages deter a particular group of children, it may be that certain schemes would not be an appropriate choice. On the other hand, there is a monetary price to be paid for the more lavish schemes and a school may legitimately decide that it cannot afford the luxury of their full-colour printing and spacious lay-out.

Teachers' materials

Most modern mathematics schemes are equipped with teachers' books in some shape or form but these vary from the extremely detailed support and guidance offered in a scheme such as *SPMG* to the rather skimpy treatment in *Mastermaths* where the provision consists chiefly of answers to the work in the children's books and some pages of activity suggestions for photocopying. The provision may even vary within a scheme as in *Step by Step* where the teacher's book to accompany the infant stage of the course is full of information, explanation and inventive ideas about additional activities for children while the books for the junior stage become progressively more parsimonious in the advice and guidance offered and focus almost exclusively on the pages of the children's books.

Teachers will, of course, vary in the amount of advice they require and some might find the detailed guidance of *Ginn*, for example, condescending while others may welcome it. One teacher's straitjacket is another's life support system. Yet any minimum concept of teachers' materials must surely include an explanation of how the parts of the scheme relate to each other and how common topics are developed throughout the scheme and it is worrying to find this apparently absent on occasions, as with *Mastermaths* and *Kites*. Teachers will also vary in their preference for format in teachers' materials. Some will find the large, multi-

The practice of including pages of children's work in the Teacher's Book helps teachers keep track of activities. (*Nuffield Maths* 1, Teachers' Handbook, p. 91.)

Sorting activities which enable the children to handle, compare and sort real objects can be carefully structured and stored in boxes.

The 'long and short' box, for example, would contain pairs of objects identical in every respect *except* length.

Two pieces of dowelling rod.
Two pencils.
Two pieces of ribbon.
Two strips of Meccano.
Two candles.
Two cardboard tubes ... etc.

The child sorts these by placing the objects on a piece of manilla divided into two sections labelled 'long' and 'short'. Later, a simple record can be made by drawing.

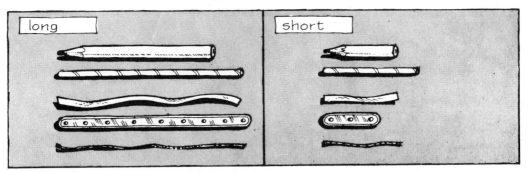

Similar boxes for 'fat and thin', 'wide and narrow', 'tall and short', can be assembled and used in the same way. It is possible to buy a set of attribute cylinders which display differences in height, length and thickness.

Worksheets should not be introduced until children have had plenty of practical experience and opportunity for discussion.

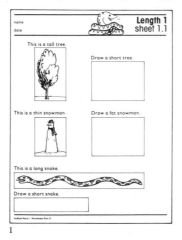

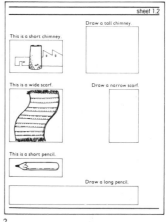

1   2

purpose teachers' books which accompany, for example, *Mathematics for Schools* reassuring, helpful and uncomplicated to use. By contrast, they may find the series of small booklets which accompanies *IMP* bitty and confusing. Others may appreciate the flexibility of *IMP* and reject the bulkiness of *Mathematics for Schools*.

It is difficult for writers of schemes to get the teachers' materials right in the first publication and it is interesting to note instances where they have been added rather late (*Beta*) or reorganised quite early in the scheme's life (*Peak*). As yet there appear to be no teachers' materials at all to accompany *Racing to Maths* and advice seems to be confined to hints for teachers on the actual pages of the children's materials and a few directions in the Answer Book.

One helpful trend that is much to be welcomed is the inclusion of reproductions of the pupils' materials within the teachers' books. This occurs for example in *Nuffield*, *Mathematics for Schools* and *Macmillan Junior Mathematics*, and makes an immediate and clear connection between what the children are doing and what the teacher may want to be doing.

Several schemes provide answers to the children's work within the teachers' books. This is the case with *Macmillan Junior Mathematics* and *Ginn*. Others like *SMP*, *Peak* and *SPMG* provide them for the junior stage in separate book form. The practice of *Racing to Maths* of providing only one book for the whole junior scheme is not helpful. There seems to be some tendency for the existence of answer books to be played down in the publicity materials for the schemes as if they are not quite respectable in a modern product. There is also a tendency to include them as part of the teachers' materials (for example *SPMG*) with the unfortunate implication that checking answers is principally the teacher's business rather than the children's. It is refreshing to see *Arnold* referring to them quite explicitly in the publicity materials and promoting them as books for both teachers and children to use.

Additional materials

Many recent schemes provide additional materials beyond the main stream teachers' and children's materials and these may be considered very important by some teachers and in some situations. A headteacher anxious to promote the microcomputer work in the school may well favour a scheme such as *Peak* or *SPMG* where computer software has been produced to dovetail with the main materials. Teachers who have used the 'big book' format in the teaching of reading and found it an effective way of providing a shared experience for a group of children may well be attracted by a scheme such as *Ginn* which provides 'big book' materials for mathematics. Of course, supplementary materials require separate evaluation. In particular, their usefulness needs to be related to their cost, which may be considerable.

Infant teachers who believe in the value of approaching learning through play may welcome the rhyme cards of *IMP* and the games to accompany the infant stage of *Step by Step*, where the bold, full-colour pictures are likely to prove instantly attractive to young children. Indeed, teachers at any level who are at all doubtful about being able to create support materials of an acceptable standard will be likely to welcome those schemes such as *Peak* and *SPMG* which do provide a pack of materials for teachers to draw upon to support the scheme.

Step by Step goes one stage further in providing the actual equipment needed at the infant level by means of an Equipment Box. The authors are sensitive to the fact that it may not be easy for teachers to obtain in precisely correct form certain features which are essential to the work envisaged. Provision is selective, however, so that the Equipment Box does not become too bulky; other more common items are merely specified.

For teachers who are particularly concerned about children's mastery of the necessary mathematical language for a successful start, the Bronto books of *Nuffield* which set out to introduce and reinforce the use of mathematical language in lively settings will be an attractive and reassuring feature.

For the most part, however, schemes make recommendations rather than provide practical support and extension materials and equipment. Almost without exception, these are listed in an appropriate place in the teachers' materials. Occasionally, as in *Mastermaths* and *SMP*, they also appear at the head of children's materials so that children can ensure that they are properly prepared before they begin work. The claim is usually made that what is needed is drawn from 'what most schools can expect to have' (*SMP*), or 'easily obtainable' (*Arnold*). This claim would appear to be largely true. The important thing would be for teachers to discover whether a scheme does make use of specialised equipment such as structural apparatus (for example *Nuffield*) or calculators (for example *SPMG*) so that steps could be taken in advance to ensure an adequate supply.

Some schemes go farther than simply listing materials which are required. *Nuffield* and *Step by Step*, for instance, are particularly helpful in this respect. *Step by Step* makes suggestions about actual storage of materials and supplies names of stockists and *Nuffield* gives advice about the making of support materials.

The scheme in use

Publishers' descriptions of schemes almost always make them sound attractive but the real test for a teacher must be how they function in the classroom. There is no better way of making this assessment than visiting a school that is actually using the scheme. Nevertheless, in a preliminary examination of a scheme there are certain features to look for which can indicate how well it will fit particular situations.

Structure and flexibility

The structure of the scheme and the degree of flexibility built into it warrant particular con-

sideration. Structure is important if teacher and children are to be able to operate the scheme purposefully, knowing what they are doing and where they are going. Flexibility is important in making it possible for teachers to adapt each child's experience to fit his or her needs, varying the amount and the type of activity and using materials from any section of the scheme as appropriate. This requirement becomes particularly critical in schools with mixed age classes or especially wide ability ranges.

It is possible for structure and flexibility to be opposing notions in that if the structure of a scheme demands that children should pass sequentially through each stage (for example *Racing to Maths*) there may not be sufficient scope for varying the amount of experience for the individual child. Fortunately in almost all schemes mentioned here, teachers are advised to divert from the core materials for the purposes of consolidation or enrichment. It may be that this is more likely to occur in practice where consolidation or enrichment materials are actually provided as part of the scheme as with *Ginn* and even more likely if there is a well signposted branching programme indicated in the children's core materials as is the case with *Arnold*. Where extension work is largely a matter of following suggestions in the teacher's book while consolidation work is actually provided as with *Mathematics for Schools*, it may be that consolidation will tend to occur more frequently than extension.

So the range of materials provided in a scheme is likely to have a strong influence on the flexibility with which the scheme is used. The type of materials forming the core of the scheme is similarly likely to influence flexibility. A scheme such as *SMP* which relies so completely on cards makes it easy to vary each child's working pattern and for any child or group of children in a school to have access to any unit of cards. Core books are less easy to pass about the school.

The question of coherence across infant and junior classes also needs to be considered. If the materials have been separately designed and are organised along different lines there may be difficulties for children in adapting from one scheme to another. There may also be some restriction on the degree of operational flexibility possible. The dangers of dislocation are clearly greatest where two separate schemes are used unless the schemes, like *IMP* and *SMP* have been designed to fit together although, even here, the approach is noticeably different. It is quite common, though, for different approaches to be used for infant and junior work even in the same scheme so that *Nuffield* adopts a worksheet format at infant level and a textbook format at junior level; *Macmillan* moves from work cards to textbooks; *Step by Step* changes the balance from largely teacher organised work at the infant level where the children's books play only a minor part to work centred on the children's books at the junior level. It can well be argued, however, that provided the sections of the scheme are compatible, diversity of approach is to be welcomed for children who are at different levels of development. Certainly dislocation does not necessarily occur and is unlikely where a scheme is sensitive to the dangers and provides for revision of infant material at lower junior level (for example *Step by Step*; *Nuffield*) and ensures coherence for the teacher, for example by adopting a common format in the teachers' books (for example *Nuffield*; *Ginn*).

Serviceability

Most of the schemes referred to provide pupils' books of an appropriate degree of durability. Some (for example *Ginn*) are stapled while others (for example *Peak*) are bound and therefore possibly longer lasting (unless something goes wrong with the binding in which case they may prove to be irreparable).

Answer books need to be particularly strong if they are to stand up to frequent consultation by children and teacher. Flimsy products like those accompanying *Step by Step* do not compare well with the more substantial books provided by *SPMG*. Consumable materials are rightly kept to a minimum level of durability in all schemes, although with *Arnold* they seem to border on the austere. Work cards must be sufficiently robust to withstand heavy use by numbers of children. For this, card of a sufficiently heavy weight must be used, the cards must be laminated and they must not be too large and consequently vulnerable to bending if they are to have a reasonable life expectancy. Cards like the *Arnold* ones are unlikely to last as long as the more substantial cards which make up *SMP* or form part of *Ginn*.

Where teachers' books are central to a scheme and therefore likely to be referred to frequently, they will need to be strong and sufficiently large to allow instant consultation. The teachers' books for *Mathematics for Schools*, *Arnold*, *Nuffield* and *Step by Step*, are particularly good in this respect and the spiral binding of the *Ginn* teacher's book which makes it lie flat on a desk has much to recommend it.

A commercial scheme must offer the prospect of smooth-running use in the classroom or it fails to fulfil one of its major functions, that of easing a teacher's organisational load. To a large extent this will depend on whether the children understand the scheme and know how to operate it, and this will be discussed elsewhere. The kind of organisation the materials lend themselves to is also important, however, and the more complex a scheme is, the more difficult it may be to devise an effective organisation which allows children to gain access, use and return materials with maximum independence. Surprisingly few schemes offer advice on this aspect of the work; *Step by Step* and *Nuffield* are among the exceptions here. Even fewer actually incorporate storage facilities into the scheme and where this does happen they tend to be either insufficiently robust for the use to which they may be subjected as with the slip cases of *Macmillan Mathematics* or insufficiently flexible to allow multiple access as with the card-boxes of *SMP*. It may be that we should look to firms other than publishers to supply the range of storage systems appropriate for modern mathematics schemes and in the meantime inventive teachers will have to continue to devise their own.

Appeal

The immediate appearance of a scheme will inevitably affect its appeal both to children and teachers. It has already been mentioned that schemes like *Ginn* and *Peak* where the children's materials are colourful and spaciously laid out may have a head start on those like *Mastermaths* and *Arnold* where economies have been made. First impressions do not always count for very much, however, and it is the content rather than the lavishness of presentation that will determine the ultimate appeal.

Perhaps of greater long-term importance is the use that is actually made of visually attractive features like photographs, pictures, diagrams, charts and colour, and this is where intensive inspection is necessary. Does the arresting photograph of a British Airways jet on pages 40 and 41 of *Peak 7* really relate to the questions which accompany it? Will the full-colour pictures in the *IMP* Rhymes and Stories pack motivate young children and focus their attention? Does the illustration of a 1 litre jug beside 10 small jugs accompanying an instruction to use a small jug to fill a larger jug clarify or confuse by pre-empting the work children are asked to do in *Arnold*, Stage One, page 155? Does a graph provide information which children might be better off gathering themselves in *Ginn*, Level 4, Textbook 2, page 23?

It is not suggested that the answer to all of the questions should be negative but simply that these are important questions to ask and that this is the level of investigation which is necessary.

Acquisition

Some schemes are actually easier for schools to acquire than others. This is partly a matter of the way in which they are marketed and partly a matter of cost.

Marketing

Most publishers offer special evaluation packs which enable teachers to try out materials and inspect them closely before purchase. Some, in addition to this, are particularly helpful in sending representatives to explain their schemes (for example *Step by Step* and *Arnold*). Some are happy to provide the names of schools already using their scheme so that visits can be made (for example *Peak*), or organise local meetings to discuss the schemes (for example *Nuffield*). Publishers of some of the schemes mentioned do all of these things. Indeed, for the majority of schemes on the market today there is little difficulty in obtaining information or ultimately delivery of the materials. It is for a teacher to be alert to the degree of impartiality in the information and advice offered and to ensure that as much as possible comes from a neutral source such as a local authority adviser or another school.

Cost

This is of the utmost importance to almost all schools contemplating purchase and here the question is not only that of the relative cost of the different schemes but also the difference in cost between having a scheme and not having one at all. The cheapest policy would undoubtedly be to purchase a single set of material from every scheme and to rework many of the excellent ideas to fit the context of a particular school.

Assuming that a school has made a decision in principle to adopt a scheme, however, cost will be determined by such factors as the range of materials, the lavishness of production and the degree of consumability involved. Most publishers are prepared to give an estimate of cost and should be asked to do so, so that comparisons can be made. It would be wise for schools also to check these estimates in the light of how they expect to use them: common access to materials may reduce costs whereas duplication at crossover points like the infant/ junior stage will make practical sense but is likely to increase them. It is also wise to consider cost in relation to how the introduction of the scheme is to be phased over the school as a whole so that the likely cost of introduction and maintenance of the scheme over a number of years can be established.

2 Aims, objectives and scope of the scheme

Aims

Despite recurrent expressions of alarm in the media concerning the purpose of teaching mathematics there is a substantial amount of agreement in primary schools about the importance of mathematics in the curriculum, although the day-to-day emphasis varies considerably within and between schools. Pressure from central and local government, combined with a developing sense of professionalism among teachers, has ensured that the vast majority of schools have, in one way or another, and to a greater or lesser degree, produced a set of aims for the mathematics curriculum. Comparison of any school's notional, or real, aims with the list developed in the HMI document *Mathematics from 5–11* (1979) and quoted on page 5 of this book is unlikely to find any serious discrepancy.

In fact it is relatively easy to produce a list of suitable aims which look impressive and include all the latest 'buzz-words'. Much more difficult is the task of refining the general aims of primary mathematics into workable long-term and short-term objectives. Strictly speaking this should be the job of the staff of a school, who then select suitable curricular materials to try to fulfil the stated aims. In reality, teachers are looking for one or more sets of materials which they hope will automatically fulfil many of the general aims. Therefore it seems logical that published schemes should themselves include statements of aims in order to encourage a match between teachers and pupils and the materials they will use.

Such aims should include, as a minimum, statements about content, teaching approaches, styles or means of learning, assessment and evaluation, and expectations concerning the affective domain of attitudes and personal qualities. Such statements should be written directly into the materials, and if they exist are likely to be found at the beginning of the teacher's handbook. The inclusion of such statements only in the sales information, or their complete omission, implies that the materials are generally suitable for all purposes, at all times and for all children. This suggestion is patently untrue and exists only in the minds of sales managers.

The extent to which published schemes provide specification of their aims varies considerably, although in most cases it is possible to infer a set of aims by examination of the style of the materials offered for use.

A comprehensive list of aims for the scheme is stated at the start of the teacher's book of, for example, *Arnold Junior Mathematics* (page 6):

1 To encourage children's confidence in their ability to understand and do mathematics.
2 To provide adequate concrete experience to allow the secure formation of concepts and the development of understanding.
3 To give sufficient practice material to ensure that the children become fluent in the basic skills.
4 To provide enough extension material to challenge the most able children.
5 To emphasise the value of verbalisation in learning mathematics.
6 To present, where appropriate, different experiences leading to the same concept.
7 To develop a flexible attitude to number work, particularly mental calculations.
8 To provide a wide range of activities in

measurement, shape and pattern as a complement to the central number work.

9 To develop a positive attitude to problem solving and open-ended work.

10 To allow all children to experience pattern in mathematics.

It is appropriate to notice the use of words and the implied emphasis. 'Concrete experience', 'developing understanding', 'basic skills', 'extension material', 'able children', 'verbalisation', 'different experiences', 'flexible attitude', 'wide range', 'central number work', 'positive attitude', 'problem solving', 'open ended work', and 'pattern' are all words currently receiving emphasis in the academic and professional literature of mathematics education. The aims are therefore weighted towards mathematical processes and attitudes of learners, although number work is regarded, quite rightly, as 'central'.

A similarly comprehensive statement is offered in the Teacher's Resource Book for *Mathematics For Schools* (page viii), where the authors write as follows:

We aim to encourage your children;
to enjoy mathematics.
to understand other aspects of mathematics as well as numeration.
to use their existing knowledge to try to solve a problem rather than to say 'we haven't done that yet'.
to think logically and analytically.
to talk about and discuss the mathematics they are doing.
to become aware of mathematics all around them.

We aim to help you (the teacher);
to plan an enjoyable, purposeful and integrated mathematics course.
to present mathematical concepts in a logical order.
to prepare carefully structured lessons.
to provide balanced practice and consolidation.
to evaluate the children's learning.

In contrast some schemes provide a very brief statement of aims, emphasising only a few aspects. *Mastermaths* (page 3), for example, offers the following:

1 To combine the best traditional mathematics with a modern, lively approach.

2 To provide a basis for class, group or individual teaching.

3 To provide as many opportunities as possible for teachers to talk usefully with their pupils. This is done by providing support for the pupils so that unnecessary interruptions are avoided.

4 To make the learning of mathematics enjoyable for children . . .

5 . . . and easy for their teachers to manage.

This is significantly less meaningful, less 'mathematical' and in reality less useful to the teacher examining a number of schemes, although superficially it uses attractive words like 'easy', 'enjoyable' and so on.

A further contrast with the full statement of some schemes is found in *Racing To Maths*, which, at the time of going to press, had no teachers' books and only the briefest statement of intent, written on the back cover of the texts. This runs as follows:

. . . continues the systematic, programmed approach begun in the Infant series. Pupils gain a firm grasp of all essential topics and confidence in handling them . . . mathematics is made real and relevant to everyday life. The needs of pupils are met. The scheme is flexible enough to create strong motivation and commendable achievement across the ability range.

Between the extremes of clarity in the statement of aims there are many attempts to set out the general purpose of a particular scheme. *Beta Mathematics* makes few overt statements about aims; the purpose of primary mathematics in general and the scheme in particular is assumed. However, the implied aim is quite clearly the development of basic 'skills' in mathematics with little attention paid to the wider aims which have been so clearly stated in the literature and in the handbooks of more modern schemes.

Step by Step pays attention to the need for statements about aims. While the aims of the scheme are set out rather differently in the teacher's books for the Infant and Junior schemes there is clear consistency of intention. This is to develop understanding and enjoyment of mathematics by relating mathematical processes to concrete situations, proceeding by means of small and logically ordered steps and by employing as many varied and enjoyable activities as possible to help children acquire essential mathematical facts.

Ginn Mathematics provides a brief statement of aims within a general overview of the wide range of materials supplied as part of the scheme. Again the 'right things' are written to reflect current thinking in educational theory and policy with regard to mathematics. *SMP*, being a card-based scheme, draws attention to the flexibility and the organisational possibilities (but not the problems) of the scheme and the aims which are specified are similar to the better offerings already discussed, although less overt in their statement.

While the stated or implied aims of a scheme should be examined to attempt a match with the needs of the school there is a problem in that statements about aims are not a guarantee that the material in use will actually encourage their achievement. Their usefulness for a teacher examining the quality of the current scheme or choosing a new scheme is that the presence of such statements implies that there may have been a sense of purpose in the writing which may enhance the scheme's continuity, consistency and style. The actual final decision about the relative importance of the aims (stated or implied) is a problem for discussion within an individual school, but should not be ignored.

Objectives

If the usual distinction between aims as long-term intentions and objectives as shorter-term, more specific intentions is adopted, then it is possible to consider whether in fact the objectives of particular books, units, sections or pages, proposed for teachers and pupils, are consistent with the aims.

As a general rule there seems to be a high level of consistency between the stated aims and the shorter-term objectives specified for most schemes. The schemes which intend to concentrate on number do in fact concentrate on this aspect in the stated headings and page titles of the materials, which closely approximate to objectives for most schemes. A particular example is *Beta* which is presumably based on developing a facility with numbers and reflects accurately the overt image of the scheme.

The more comprehensive schemes, however, have taken the statement of objectives to a much more precise degree which might provide a model for all good schemes which are intended to constitute a full course of teaching and learning primary mathematics. A common view of objectives in education is that they should be stated behaviourally, that is in terms of what the learner should be able to do, make or perform after completing the work on a particular section or page. This implies that the objectives should be stated in such a way that we can assess whether the intention has been achieved. More recent views are that objectives should include items concerned with the *process* of learning in addition to the definition of ends.

Ginn Mathematics, *Arnold Junior Mathematics*, and *Mathematics For Schools*, are examples of schemes which have taken the idea of an objectives-based approach to a highly systematic level. However the idea is not dealt with rigidly. Indeed, to attempt to state the whole sequence of the primary mathematics curriculum in behavioural terms would be an unwieldy and over-formal gesture and would reduce the possibilities for flexibility and creativity in both teaching and learning. Consequently they have all softened the approach to include such objectives as 'to enable children to investigate tessellations'. This is a mathematically valid activity, is capable of assessment at the 'yes they have!' level, and is able to be related directly to the stated or implied aims of the scheme and of the school.

Ginn Mathematics, therefore, is able on consecutive pages of the Teacher's Resource Book (but not the pupils' book) to state objectives like these

Level 6, Textbook 1, Page 30:

To enable the children to:
evaluate expressions using brackets and the four operations;
solve problems based on the above.

Level 6, Textbook 1, Page 31:

To enable children to:
practise division by means of a game;
improve their knowledge of place value.

All the objectives of a particular level are stated in sequence at the start of the Teacher's Resource Book, although they are stated without subheadings and consequently without any suggestion of interrelationships.

Arnold Junior Mathematics is slightly more precise. The scheme is structured to encourage teachers and pupils to undertake several pages of work on a particular topic. The Teacher's Book 1 is therefore subheaded on page 61:

Topic 9. Weight
Aims
To introduce the kilogram (kg) and the hectogram (hec).
To identify objects which are lighter or heavier than a kilogram.
To estimate and weigh in hectograms (hecs).
To establish that 10 hecs = 1 kg.

Notice the use of the term 'Aims' when in fact these are short-term objectives. Clearly the arbitrary use of terms could lead to confusion as indeed could the combination of objectives for teaching as well as learning.

Mathematics For Schools takes the idea one step further. The Teacher's Resource Books, and the pupils' books are divided into sections. The Teacher's Resource Book for Levels 1 and 2 has a section entitled, for example

'Length'. The objectives of the section are stated as follows (page 12):

To consolidate and develop children's ideas about the use of standard units in the measurement of length.
To develop children's concept of length, including that of perimeter and shortest distance.
To enable children to relate their number work in addition and difference to the measurement of length and to give them practice with basic number facts.
To enable children to discover a simple relationship between the circumference and the diameter of a circle.

Pages of the pupils' book are then grouped under more precise objectives, called in this scheme 'purposes'. The first examples are as follows (page 14):

To re-inforce the children's ideas about the need for a standard unit of measure: the metre.
To enable the children to appreciate the idea of perimeter.
To give the children further practice in the use of sub-units of a metre.

'Check-ups' are provided to allow formal or informal assessment of the level of achievement of the children.

Such statements of objectives provide a very useful guide to the sequence of a scheme in terms of its content and the achievements to be expected from the pupils. The scheme makes it absolutely clear why a lesson or page of work is being undertaken.

Less precise, but possibly no less useful, is the practice adopted in *Macmillan Junior Mathematics* and in *SPMG*. In these the Teacher's Book contains statements which approximate to informally stated objectives. For example, the authors of *Macmillan Junior Mathematics* Teacher's Notes, Level 1, page 10 entitle a section 'Content' and write:

Adding 9 successively so that the total does not exceed 100. At each stage the sum of the digits is found.

This is the content 'objective' for a single page.

In *SPMG* pages are grouped together, with statements such as

Stage 4, part 2 (page 26):

> Vulgar Fractions.
> Content.
> The number work of this section revises the concept of vulgar fractions and equivalent fractions. The remaining pages deal with the addition and subtraction of fractions less than one.

In addition each of these schemes provides a title or sub-title for each page which states quite specifically what is being learned, for example 'Adding 9' (*Macmillan Junior Mathematics*, Book 1A, page 18), or 'Making Equal Fractions' (*SPMG*, Stage 4, page 25).

Other schemes are less specific about the objectives of the pages or sections. While this may not reduce the validity of the work offered to teachers and children it does make it more difficult to decide upon specific sequences of work suitable for particular classes or pupils since the teacher is forced to decide about the purpose of the page or section and how it might fit (or not) with a required programme of learning.

The statements of aims and objectives, or lack of them, in the various schemes tend to imply a particular approach to teaching and learning. This question will be considered in more detail later, but it is clear that the authors of the schemes adopt a particular general stance with regard to their own material, some seeing the scheme as a flexible resource to be 'picked over' by a teacher, others seeing the scheme as a rather rigid framework for use in strict order at particular stages.

This also implies an emphasis, or not, on teacher direction of the children's learning or on child self-direction. While all schemes are designed so that teachers control the sequence and pace of learning some schemes are more suitable than others for one or other of the general styles. For example, *SMP* is specified as being for children working 'in the main, either individually or in small groups' (Teacher's Handbook, page 4). On the other hand *Peak*, in Junior Handbook 1 (page 9) states that 'it cannot be emphasised too strongly that the success of the scheme depends upon the teacher's involvement, both in the teaching of the skills and the provision, where necessary, of supplementary material'.

As a contrast, *Racing To Maths* offers no advice to the teacher about his or her role. In fact the layout of the pages and the inclusion of a large element of 'teaching' on most pages implies that the pupil is able to work unaided on the material. However, the highly concise nature of the scheme would make self-direction impossible for all but the brightest children.

The more comprehensive schemes have attempted to provide aspects of both teacher direction and pupil direction of learning. Some, like *Ginn Mathematics*, *Arnold Junior Mathematics*, *Maths Adventure*, and *SPMG* provide supplementary texts or cards which allow a teacher to direct the bulk of the children's learning, but also include workbooks, reproducible worksheets, and/or workcards which would allow a child to proceed at his or her own pace for at least part of the course.

General content, approach and activities

Teachers often trust the authors and publishers of a scheme to deliver what they promise in their statements of aims and objectives. Evaluating whether in fact the general content, approach and activities are consistent with the stated intentions is only possible when a scheme has been used for a long time with a large number of pupils.

Clearly, therefore, a degree of specification of the general content, approach and activities would be of great value to a busy teacher, not only for long-term evaluation but also for making valid and purposeful use of the materials on a day-to-day basis. It would be helpful to have the mathematical concepts, skills and generalisations clearly identified for each topic being taught and learned, and also for each small section or page. Whether or not this is stated, the suggested activities should link clearly with the stated objectives so that the teacher knows exactly what the children are doing and why.

At a practical level, a scheme should indicate clearly whether special materials or facilities are required, especially with regard to the grouping of children and the extent to which they will work 'outside' or with messy or dangerous materials. Similarly, there should be clear specification of the type and range of equipment to be used, especially if commercially produced structural apparatus is to be used, like Dienes' Multibase Arithmetic Blocks, or Cuisenaire Rods.

The published schemes vary considerably in their ability to offer this sort of information which is so essential for valid planning of the curriculum at the practical level, and which to a large extent determines the ease of use of the scheme.

For example, in *SMP*, the mathematical content of each Unit is concisely set out. However, the modular structure of the material minimises the opportunities for interrelating the various clusters of concepts, except in the later Units which reduce the number of topics and use more integrated activities. A small amount of information is offered concerning arrangement of materials, classroom organisation, marking and recording. However, it is general in tone and while reinforcing the emphasis on flexibility of use does not offer specific advice at times when it might be needed, for example with measurement activities in the topic of 'Capacity'.

The actual approach to learning is highly specified by the cards themselves. The only curricular flexibility, apart from omitting or rearranging certain sections, arises from the provision of two separate strands for the teaching of place value and addition, one based specifically on the use of multibase blocks and the other using the traditional abacus/base 10 mode. It is not made clear, either to the teacher or the child, what methods of calculation are to be used. Nor is

the purpose, rather than the content, of any module specified. However, in general the required equipment is simple, generally available, and easy to use. Suggested activities are realistic and generally take place within the confines of the school. Activities are varied, but if children work as individuals or in small groups supervision by the teacher could become a problem.

Beta offers a similar, but book-based, amount of information. The mathematical concepts and skills are clearly set out and grouped according to topic and shown on the contents page. In addition, each page carries a heading which identifies the concept or skill with which the page is chiefly concerned. The Teacher's Manual also shows how the contents of all six books are linked under the headings of Number and Money, Measures, Fractions, Sets, Time, Graphs, Lines, Angles and Shapes, Surfaces and Solids, and Plans and Maps. The teacher is briefly informed about the required equipment and facilities but left to his or her own devices about the choice, extent and provision of further activities. The purpose of the specified activities is therefore perhaps clear to the teacher but not necessarily to the child since he is seldom offered a reason for what he is asked to do.

The suggested activities are always relevant to the topic but are not always consistent with the accepted beliefs about how children learn. Practical work plays a relatively minor part in the scheme, most time being devoted to consolidation and practice of skills, often at a mechanical level. Where children are involved in practical activities these are most frequently of the desk top kind. Clearly these are simple to organise and demand little in the way of special resources and facilities. In consequence there is a considerable restriction on the range of materials, apparatus and approaches with which a child is likely to have experience.

In contrast, *Mathematics For Schools*, *Ginn Mathematics* and *SPMG* specify the mathematical concepts and skills which are relevant at each stage of the scheme by stating clear objectives and providing an outline of the concepts which are at issue. These are related to previous experiences and clear suggestions are made for further use and elaboration. It is thus made clear how a current activity fits into the overall pattern of the scheme and what it is hoped will be achieved from it.

The general approach to be adopted for each topic is set out in the Teacher's Books and recommendations are made about methods of calculation to be used. This clearly reduces flexibility and, if the teaching suggestions are used, along with the supplementary materials, there is little real scope for teachers to deviate from the recommended methods without risking inconsistency or loss of direction. Indeed, if all the prescriptions are followed, then every step of the whole course is laid out in detail. The schemes make no unusual demands in relation to space, resources or grouping. However, despite the fact that the schemes are geared to a system of use with small, ability based groups it is clear that a fair quantity of class based teaching and learning will be required.

Scope

Almost all published schemes for use in primary schools claim to be comprehensive. Each sales pamphlet, and indeed each teacher's book where available, suggests that the materials supplied are sufficient to cater for the needs of all except the least able children. *SMP* suggests that 'the very able, average, and less able children are well catered for. It should be suitable for a broad range of ability within a class, but the very slow or remedial child will need extra help' (Teacher's Handbook, page 4). Some, like *Mathematics For Schools, Arnold Junior Mathematics* and *Ginn Mathematics* make a deliberate point of supplying ideas and/or curricular materials for extension and enrichment of the curriculum. The scheme published by Schofield and Sims is divided into two mini-schemes, *Alpha* for 'children of good average and above average ability', and *Beta* for 'children of average and below average ability'.

Whether a scheme will fit the definition of ability in a particular geographical region depends on circumstances and on the personal views of the teacher.

All schemes specify the age range for which the materials have been designed, although care needs to be taken because the range varies:

e.g. Alpha and Beta (7–13)
Time for Maths (5–7)
Mathematics For Schools Level 1 (5–7)
Mathematics For Schools Level 2 (7–13)
Moore's Maths For Infants (5–7)
Arnold Junior Mathematics (7–11)
Peak (5–13)
Macmillan Junior Mathematics (7–11)
SMP (7–13)
Nuffield (5–12)
Step by Step (4–13)

The different target age ranges would need particular attention in regions with combinations of Infant and Junior, Primary, First, Middle and Combined schools, and also those with nursery units attached.

Whether or not the teacher wishes to use a single published scheme as the only mathematics materials in a school or classroom, it is essential to be able to see the way in which the content is structured and inter-related. Different schemes use different ways in which to show this, generally using one or more of these modes; matrix charts, a cross-referenced index, concept groupings or flow diagrams. Because a scheme is fundamentally a resource for planning mathematical education it is important that such a framework should be illuminating and easy to understand for a busy teacher, as well as being an accurate guide to the structure of the primary mathematics that is offered in the scheme.

The standard practice appears to be the production of a 'scope and sequence chart' which, for each book, level or stage lists the topics to be covered. Some schemes provide notes on two or three of the consecutive stages or books so that a broader sweep is achieved. Attempts to provide a chart with an overview of the whole of primary mathematics are either doomed to excessive complexity or are too concise to show the sort of detail required by teachers.

Mathematics For Schools uses a combination of the matrix chart and the cross-referenced index, listing in detail the pages in consecutive pairs of books which contain material under the following headings:

Numeration

Sets and Subsets
Addition
Subtraction
Position Value
Multiplication
Division
Fractions and Decimals

Consolidation

Pattern

Sequential
Number

Relations

Non-numerical
Numerical

Pictorial Representation

Collecting and studying data
Using a number line

Measurement

Mass
Length
Capacity
Time and Speed
Volume
Area
Money

Shape

Solid shapes
Plane shapes
Symmetry
Angles

Ginn uses a similar format under the headings of:

General concepts of numbers
Operations with whole numbers
Fractions and decimals
Measurement
Money
Shape
Graphical representation
Problem solving

In this scheme three consecutive 'levels' are shown in the Teacher's Book for each level.

Somewhat simpler are the scope and sequence charts of *Arnold Junior Mathematics*, *Peak*, *Alpha* and *Beta* and *SMP*. These use the same style of subheadings and briefly list the activities and curricular content but omit the page numbers. The lack of page numbers makes it more difficult to move directly to a page of either the Teacher's Book or the Pupils' Book (or Card). It is necessary to refer to the index of each level in order to find the particular topic.

Simpler still is the scope and sequence chart of *Macmillan Junior Mathematics* which simply lists the page numbers, specifies the overall topic about which the page deals, and offers a brief statement about the aspect on which the teacher and children will work. However, as with *Alpha* and *Beta*, the concepts are clearly grouped to facilitate some flexibility in the sequencing.

In contrast, *Maths Adventure*, *Racing To Maths* and *Mastermaths* offer only an index to each book with some rather brief titles for each page. Determining the scope of the scheme in any sort of detail is therefore a daunting task for a teacher not fully conversant with the overall structure of mathematics. Although these later examples of schemes are perhaps easier to understand, they are less likely to provide the level of illumination required to encourage effective mathematics teaching.

Mathematics Counts (1982), The Cockcroft Report has provided the teaching profession with a model of good practice in the development of mathematical knowledge, and might be regarded as the definitive guide for what should be taught and learned and how it should be done effectively. It is likely, therefore, that all schemes published since 1982 will be at the very least paying lip service to the main recommendations of the Report. Most will be attempting to reflect them, or preferably implementing them in detail.

It should be noted, however, that the Cockcroft Report was in fact itself an analysis of current and previous good practice. Therefore it seems likely that some schemes published before 1982 will contain activities which are in accordance with the Cockcroft recommendations and earlier schemes should not necessarily be dismissed simply because of the date of publication.

The fundamental summary paragraph of the Report (paragraph 243) is worth repeating and states that:

Mathematics teaching at all levels should include opportunities for

exposition by the teacher;

discussion between teacher and pupils and between the pupils themselves;

appropriate practical work;

consolidation and practice of fundamental skills and routines;

problem solving, including the application of mathematics to everyday situations;

investigational work.

When choosing a scheme, therefore, a basic question to be answered is that of the extent to which the supplied materials and the activities they contain include opportunities for each of these aspects of mathematical education. The published schemes vary considerably in the emphasis placed on each of these aspects of 'good practice' and therefore choice of a particular scheme is likely to determine the frequency with which a teacher can provide opportunities for, say, practical work or discussion. Given widespread acceptance of these recommendations by those with power and influence in the profession, it might be a wise decision to choose a scheme which closely reflects the recommendations, while possessing other characteristics which are attractive to a particular school.

The more comprehensive and recent schemes are clearly more likely to match the recommendations. For example, *Ginn Mathematics* is careful to include opportunities for the full range of activities suggested in the Cockcroft Report. Teachers are advised on the way to introduce and develop a topic, including suitable questions to ask to stimulate discussion (although this is mainly led by the teacher rather than among the children themselves) and ideas about how practical work should be set up. It is noticeable, however, that the recommendations for practical activities decline in the later levels of the scheme. The children's core materials provide opportunities for consolidation, practice, and, by the provision of enrichment cards, for a degree of problem solving and investigational work.

An interesting point is that *Mathematics For Schools* similarly provides an almost complete reflection of the Cockcroft recommendations, although it was first published some 16 years ago! Also *Maths Adventure* encourages all the aspects by implication in the very brief teacher's notes which accompany the scheme. It is therefore unfortunate that the scheme has a very underdeveloped Teacher's Book which could have integrated the materials in the pupils' books, the activity books and the cards and, notwithstanding the other characteristics of the materials, provided a good basis for the wider approach to primary mathematics suggested by Cockcroft.

Other more recent schemes are able to make direct mention of the Cockcroft recommendations and therefore attempt to increase the credibility of the materials. *Arnold Junior Mathematics* goes as far as to spell out exactly how the scheme relates, point by point, to the Cockcroft recommendations and emphasises the value of the newer aspects like problem solving, investigations and purposeful discussion. The links are in fact backed by real advice to teachers and children and, as in *Ginn Mathematics* and *Mathematics For Schools*, the advice is complemented by the provision of suitable materials.

A similar direct link with Cockcroft is made

in *Macmillan Junior Mathematics* and, despite the compact nature of the materials, most of the recommendations are reflected directly in the design of the materials for teachers and pupils particularly with regard to discussion, problem solving and investigational approaches. It is unfortunate, therefore, that in the 1985 edition of the Teacher's Notes the name Cockcroft is written as Cockroft throughout its pages!

SMP, a pre-Cockcroft scheme, being card based, provides an unspecified but possible, direct link with the Report. The pupils' materials are the whole basis of the scheme, and therefore opportunities for exposition, and for teacher–pupil and pupil–pupil discussion would need to be created by the teacher. They are not specified overtly in the materials although clearly they would arise naturally, at least in the marking of the work from the cards. Assuming that children work through the Units at the required speed, and that marking is constructive, then children will cover all the basics of mathematics and will have experience of practical work, consolidation and practice, and to a much lesser degree, problem solving and open-ended investigation. The extent to which Units, Modules or Sections are foreshortened or emphasised depends on the teacher.

On the other hand, some recent schemes pay only lip service to the recommendations, implicitly or explicitly. For example, *Peak* is designed to offer wide coverage of primary mathematics. However, some topics, particularly aspects of measurement, are dealt with lightly in the earlier books. Nevertheless, by the end of the course, most children could have a sound armoury of mathematical skills, knowledge of conceptual structures and an ability to relate their knowledge to practical situations. The lack of adequate guidance for the teacher could, however, as in *SMP*, possibly lead to an excessive reliance on the pupils' books and a narrowing of the actual work experienced.

Other schemes apparently make no effort to offer the range of opportunities suggested by Cockcroft, although in some cases this is because they were originally conceived prior to the revolution in the style and tone of primary mathematics. *Mastermaths*, first published in 1984, makes no mention of the recommendations, and although it offers some excellent Black Line Masters as supplementary enrichment sheets, it is fundamentally concerned with developing facility with numbers. *Alpha* and *Beta*, first published almost 20 years ago, recommend a considerable amount of exposition by the teacher. Sometimes discussion between teacher and pupils is suggested but seldom is there any advocation of discussion among pupils. Provision is made for practical work but there is a large emphasis on pencil and paper work which does not require movement from the desk. Consolidation and practice of fundamental routines and skills is the most substantial element of the books, little time being accorded to genuine problem solving in real situations or to investigational work. The emphasis on the manipulation of numbers is likely to result in a high level of skill development but less certain formation of conceptual structures and the mastery of general strategies.

The Teacher's Book for *Hey, Mathematics* states quite clearly on the first page that 'it should be emphasised that much of today's primary mathematics is not considered suitable for a child's text or workbook (i.e. practical mathematics); therefore the authors have concentrated on those previously acquired basic skills that need consolidation through repetition but in a variety of ways.' However, ideas for preparatory and follow-up work using structural apparatus are briefly provided as resource material in the Teacher's Book.

Further contrast with the recommendations of the Cockcroft Report is exhibited by the recently published *Racing To Maths*. Without a teacher's book there is no means of offering advice to teachers about the teaching required for effective learning and the children's books offer few opportunities for discussion, practical work or problem solving, although the later books do offer a few rather interesting starting points for investigational work. However, these topics are not supported by the essential guidance for teachers, or indeed for the children.

Other essential questions concern the degree to which the schemes refer to up-to-date circumstances at home and in society to which children can relate; the extent to which the materials offered to children support the suggested approach to teaching; and the priority which is attached to aspects of the mathematics curriculum at the various levels, in terms of content, type and range of basic skills, the development of conceptual structures and the development of general strategies for approaching mathematical problems. Also, because of an increased awareness of the possibilities for linking mathematics with other subjects it is worth examining schemes for suggestions and/or overt links which would enrich each of the subjects involved.

The problem of being up-to-date in the examples, illustrations and general style is significant. The most recent schemes include illustrations and name children in ways which emphasise the multicultural nature of many urban areas. The emphasis on boys in illustrations and examples in earlier schemes has for the most part been noted and great care is generally taken to ensure that pupils are presented with a balanced, but necessarily rather neutral, middle-of-the-road view of life. For example, in *Step by Step* efforts have been made to select situations and examples, particularly in the pupils' books, which refer to everyday life as children in the late 1980s are likely to experience it. Thus it includes consideration of football teams, pop groups, television programmes and the like.

A similar attempt to produce relevant situations is shown in *SMP*. Although the illustrations are now looking rather dated, the situations refer generally to the everyday life of an average, normal child. Most children will therefore be able to identify with the work done to some degree although situations do tend to be neutral with regard to cultural differences.

Particular examples worthy of note are the *Alpha* and *Beta* schemes. Because of their emphasis on number skills the schemes do not draw from everyday situations. Indeed the books have a timeless quality and could easily fit into any type of society at any time in the last 30 years. In contrast, *Peak Mathematics* is firmly fixed into the 1980s. Because of the full-colour format and the use of photographs on almost every page of the earlier books, they tend to reflect a particularly contemporary socio-economic structure. This carries with it the danger that at the fashion level alone, the scheme may appear to date rapidly. Perhaps the timeless quality of *Alpha* and *Beta* is the answer for many teachers but most will probably choose something in the middle ground. Drawings date less quickly than photographs, and such schemes as *SPMG* and *Nuffield* make good use of two, four or full-colour illustrations to make the books not only generally attractive in design but also to provide identifiable characters who are capable of being 'identified with' by children. A particular example of a scheme which takes good advantage of a real situation is *Maths Adventure* which, despite the use of some rather old-fashioned line drawings, makes excellent use of a conversational style related to clearly identifiable girls, boys and various aged relatives!

At a more mathematical level, however, it is essential that the situations, illustrations and style are interesting in order to provide motivation through relevance, rather than simply to make the pages attractive. It is quite easy to say that practical work or discussion is important, and follow it by showing pictures of children working, and then to offer pupils materials which merely offer exposition and consolidation of skills with no opportunity to discuss or extend thinking.

Schemes such as *Mathematics For Schools* are particularly strong on the clarification (for teachers at least) of the overall structure and linkages of concepts and of the general strategies for approaching mathematical work. Along with *Arnold Junior Mathematics*, *Macmillan Junior Mathematics*, *SPMG* and *Ginn*,

Children may find it a help to be able to identify with established characters conversing in recognisable situations. (*Maths Adventure*, Pupil's Book 4, p. 76.)

The Tank Battle

'Ah, model tanks,' said Uncle Harry. 'I remember it all, the dust, the hot sun, the palm trees and me in the leading tank, giving orders, shouting directions, encouraging the men!'
'But you told us you were a cook in the army,' protested the boys.

'Napoleon said an army marches on its stomach,' grinned Uncle Harry.
'Nuts to Napoleon, we order our tanks using vectors,' they said.

Mathematics For Schools offers material which is directly in accord with the suggested approach to teaching. The full range of activities is included and offers a quite well-balanced diet with plenty of discussion and/or co-operation suggested. However, it is only 'suggested', and the extent to which the possibilities are utilised depends on the individual teacher.

Rarely overtly suggested in any schemes apart from *IMP*, are the possibilities for linking the work in mathematics with work in other subjects such as geography, science, craft, sport, history and so on, either singly or in interdisciplinary form. Nevertheless, many pages of the pupils' and teachers' books contain valid activities concerned with, for example, scale, map-making, co-ordinates, time zones, angles and surveying, analysis of sports results, simple experiments in physical and biological sciences, pattern-making, tessellation and symmetry. A detailed analysis of this aspect is beyond the scope of this book and would have a purpose only for those teachers who wish to develop a particular cross-curricular skill in a particular situation. However, particular strength in this is shown in such schemes as *Mathematics For Schools*, *Ginn Mathematics*, *Macmillan Junior Mathematics* and *SPMG*.

Sequence

As was suggested in the discussion of Aims and Objectives, it would be possible to analyse each scheme as it compares with a theoretically or empirically determined list or sequence of skills and content. However, the number of subskills involved and the interrelated, hierarchical nature of skill development in mathematics would produce an impossibly complex situation. Also differing views on the exact sequence in which a topic should be taught (and learned) mean that in the case of most schemes there could never be full agreement that the particular sequence or hierarchy offered was the correct one.

Consequently in choosing a scheme it would be more profitable to take a more general view and examine the extent to which the published schemes exhibit characteristics which the theoretical substructure of mathematics and the fruits of experience would suggest are sound. The important characteristics of sequencing are as follows:

1 The extent to which the approach is 'spiral', returning continually to previous situations and problems to re-examine them in the light of extended knowledge.
2 The extent to which the sequence is designed to show interrelationships within

mathematics, or conversely to concentrate on the reinforcement of skills. Both are important, but the former is essential if valid transfer of learning and use of skills is to be achieved.

3 The extent to which the presentation of concepts and skills in the children's books is clear, valid and logical.

Each of these characteristics determines the degree of flexibility of use of the scheme. The ideal situation is that of being provided with a clearly defined and stated sequence with preceding skills and knowledge specified, and the links between various topics at different levels highlighted. At the simplest organisational level this would allow easy integration of new children into the scheme, but would also allow a child who required remedial attention, or an acceleration of learning, to be correctly placed. Lack of such information places a considerable burden on the individual teacher and tends to force him or her to make intuitive decisions which are likely to produce variable levels of success.

Perhaps the most effective type of sequencing is shown by schemes which make clear statements, in their organisation and design, about the order in which topics should be covered. *Arnold Junior Mathematics* is a case in point. In this scheme the content in each book is arranged under topic headings which always follow the same sequence, commencing with place value, moving through the computational processes of addition, subtraction, multiplication and division, and completing the process with the practical topics of pattern, money, length, time, fraction, mass and weighing, volume, capacity, area and shape. Within each book, and therefore each stage, the sequence is repeated three times, roughly corresponding to one term's work, so that the approach is spiral. Flexibility is added by allowing the practical topics to be completed in almost any order. The number of topics which precede the practical sections relate to the skills required for the numerical aspects of the practical work and thus provide conceptual stepping stones for all the activities. In this way relevant practice and consolidation are achieved in realistic situations. To a large extent such a sequence also encourages the observation and use of linkages and interrelationships between the topics so that by the later stages much more generalised and less skill-specific activities can be undertaken.

A similar format is adopted by *SMP*. The whole scheme consists of six units, roughly approximating to one for each year. Each unit is divided into three Sections, roughly one for each term, and each section is divided into about eight modules or topics. The children are expected to work through the course section by section, not going on to a new section until the previous one has been completed. However, the modules can be worked in any order, thus allowing flexibility. Unfortunately, this extra flexibility can mean that a child may be working on practical activities for which the pre-requisite arithmetical abilities are underdeveloped. Extreme flexibility may therefore have its price! A system of short assessment tests may, however, allow an easier placement of a new child where this may be more difficult in a book bound system like *Arnold Junior Mathematics*.

Some other schemes are rather less precise in their organisation, and although implicitly encouraging the observation and use of interrelationships within mathematics in the later books, are more difficult to use by the teacher who wishes to design the primary curriculum to clearly exploit the interrelationship. Thus, while schemes such as *Arnold Junior Mathematics* and *SMP* clearly encourage both the development of interrelationships and consolidation/re-inforcement of learning, less compartmentalised schemes tend to concentrate more on re-inforcement. Children may therefore achieve a reduced understanding of the 'wholeness' of mathematics.

An example is *SPMG* which divides each book roughly into four parts. Each contains four to six topics, although the same topics do not arise in each part. The order in which the topics are presented is not consistent and they vary significantly in length and depth of treatment. Thus, although all topics are revisited regularly, not all are given equal importance.

A similar format is found in *Macmillan Junior Mathematics*. In Book 2 of this scheme seven sections deal with number, three sections are included for each of Area, Shape and Time, and the rest of the topics each have two 'visits'. The approach is therefore spiral, although not as clearly stated as in the other examples and the overall aim of consolidation and reinforcement is apparently emphasised. However, the whole tone and detailed content of the scheme is in fact clearly designed to show and use the interrelationships within mathematics, so first appearances can be deceptive. A similar tendency can be observed in *Mathematics For Schools*.

In contrast, the design and organisation of some schemes make it difficult to see clearly either the interrelationships or the places where reinforcement of learning is being emphasised. *Maths Adventure* provides little in the way of help and even the 'table of contents' is written as a series of rather cryptic, jokey headings (such as 'Unlucky Farmer Harry' and 'More Than You') which tell teachers or children little about the detailed content. *Peak* and *Racing To Maths*, while repeating topics at uneven intervals throughout the scheme, make little mention of the overall structure and interrelationships of mathematics.

Beta includes a number of common topics which are expanded and developed throughout the scheme. Provision is made to return to previous specific operations from time to time but this seems to be generally for the purpose of consolidating basic knowledge and skills rather than to enrich or widen knowledge and refine the mathematical approach previously used. These repetitive practices are designed to increase accuracy and speed and to develop a facility in mental arithmetic. While this is a valid aim, it tends to cloud other equally important aims such as problem solving techniques and practical skills. In general, the sequence and presentation of ideas in the children's books is clear and logical, as it is in most of the other schemes (although in *Peak* the pace of expected development of number skills is rather erratic) and it is recommended that the order of presentation in the books is strictly adhered to. No particular facilities are offered for integrating new children into the scheme but since emphasis is placed on skills there would seem to be no reason why a child could not start from a mid-point once an assessment of his skills had been made.

Some schemes, such as *Ginn Mathematics*, do in fact make a particular point of supplying test materials to allow placement of a new child. However, because each scheme has its own style, it would seem to be a suitable strategy to place all new children on a lower level than is indicated by a test until he or she is fully conversant with the style of the scheme. This would probably be particularly important with the less specific schemes such as *Maths Adventure, Mastermaths, Racing To Maths, Peak* and *Alpha/Beta*.

3 The scheme in relation to teachers

Mathematics is an essential part of the curriculum and is a subject which, because of its demands in terms of time and equipment, as well as in terms of teacher knowledge and skill, needs to be supported by resources which can help a teacher to teach and organise the curriculum as well as helping the children to learn. It is probable that the choice of a scheme will be a school decision (although the LEA, through its expert advisers, may possibly exert pressures which rather limit the choices), and therefore the chosen scheme must mediate between the various strengths and weaknesses of particular teachers. The final choice is therefore a matter for serious negotiation because it is crucial that all the teachers in a school personally feel comfortable with the scheme or schemes to be used and, if possible, actually enjoy teaching mathematics!

In the section on Design, Production and Provision it was briefly shown how the materials available for teachers and pupils vary considerably in quantity, quality and usefulness. While not implying a devaluation of the importance of sound pupil materials, including computer software, it seems likely that a teacher's book must be regarded as an essential item to be included with a scheme. A 'good' teacher's book can greatly improve the use of inadequate pupil materials by filling the gaps with sound teaching ideas, but may also be an important source of help in enhancing the teacher's own mathematical knowledge, skills and attitude as well as his or her management skills in both classroom and school. It is therefore worthwhile to consider those brief summaries of available teacher-based materials in rather more detail with some more examples, and also to consider how the use of the scheme as a whole, including the pupils' materials and the various other resources available, affect teachers.

Despite the stress, by the publishers and authors in their introductions to the schemes and in the promotional literature, on the universal validity of their materials and their apparent belief that they have produced the definitive mathematics scheme, none of the schemes in fact provides evidence properly to substantiate their suggested approach to teaching and learning. Most schemes published since 1982, particularly *Macmillan Junior Mathematics* and *Arnold Junior Mathematics*, make statements about the extent to which the schemes relate to the recommendations listed in *Mathematics Counts* (The Cockcroft Report). However, a government report is not evidence, merely a reflection of observed good practice. The substantial body of theoretical perspectives offered by Piaget, Bruner, Gagné, Dienes, Skinner, Skemp and others is not overtly stated, although of course it will have often formed the basis of the ideas of the authors. Similarly, the extensive research, by these people and many others, into ways in which children learn mathematical concepts and skills is not generally acknowledged by the authors, at least at the overt level.

However, many teachers simply do not have the time, or the interest, to substantiate their approach to the mathematics curriculum in this way and it is therefore usually necessary to assume theoretical validity and to examine materials in a more practical way. Of crucial interest is the extent to which schemes provide clear advice which will aid or enhance the teaching of a topic. Few primary school teachers have the opportunity to teach continually throughout the whole age range and therefore develop a wide and deep knowledge of suitable techniques for all topics and stages of development. However, most teachers change the age group taught at some time, and some find themselves teaching a new age group every couple of years. It is therefore helpful to many to be offered clear curricular advice about techniques for teaching a topic, information about essential, or at least suitable, materials and equipment to be used and, if possible, some indication of the mathematical background to the children's activities, written at the teacher's level. We will consider aspects of classroom management later.

Apart from the few schemes, like *Racing To Maths*, which do not have a teacher's book and therefore offer minimal help and advice to the teacher, these three essential items appear, to a greater or lesser degree, in most schemes. However, the emphasis given to each aspect varies considerably.

For example, *Mathematics For Schools* is very much a scheme for the 'teaching' of mathematics. Each topic in the Teacher's Resource Book is preceded by a concisely written section setting out the mathematical background to the topic at the particular level being considered, making full use of diagrammatic representations, and relating it to work done at previous levels. Notes are offered regarding the direction of future work on the specified and cognate topics. Suitable teaching aids are briefly listed, although names and addresses of suitable suppliers of materials are omitted. However, most of the suggested items are easily obtainable, such as boxes of pebbles, string and the like.

A significant level of advice is offered about ways to teach the topic. The pages of the pupils' books are reproduced in the Teacher's Resource Book so that the latter can be related to the former directly and easily. For each topic the correct mathematical vocabulary is listed, with examples, so that if used in conjunction with the section dealing with the mathematical background accurate terminology is introduced and reinforced. Teachers are then offered a number of introductory activities which are designed to constitute the teacher–exposition and discussion. This is followed by descriptions of suitable ways to actually 'teach the page' of the pupils' book. Each section concludes with suggestions for follow-up activities and ideas for enrichment and broadening of the child's experience, although here the onus is on the teacher to design, produce and implement the actual activity. The answers are in a separate booklet.

Nuffield Mathematics and *SPMG* adopt a similar approach, offering advice about equipment and vocabulary. There is relatively little offered in the way of mathematical background for teachers. However, the 'working with the children' sections are broadly based and quite comprehensive in their treatment of the particular topic at the particular level. Indeed, in *Nuffield* at least, the notes go well beyond the information required simply to teach the pages to the child. Clear advice is also offered about the design and construction of apparatus and visual aids, and each section concludes with a list of references and resources which are available from other publishers and educational suppliers.

Arnold Junior Mathematics, *Macmillan Junior Mathematics* and *Ginn Mathematics* each lay great emphasis on their recent date of publication and make much use of the recommendations of the Cockcroft Report in their sales material and indeed in the teachers' books to show how they might reflect the recommendations. For each topic the schemes include a concise list of equipment to be used and a set of concise, but easy to understand, notes about the introduction and development of the topic.

One of the claims of most recent schemes, especially noticeable in the publicity material of *Ginn Mathematics*, is that the materials set high standards of what might be called 'teachability'. Presumably this means that the scheme is easy to use for teaching mathematics. In fact, like *Mathematics For Schools*, the authors ensure that teachers receive a clear list of objectives for the section, topic or page which help teachers to understand both what they are trying to achieve and what is expected to be achieved in other parts of the scheme.

Such information would certainly ease the problems of teaching an unfamiliar topic.

However, each of these schemes offers only a cursory amount of information about the mathematical background to the topic (at an adult level) which forces teachers to rely on the offered techniques without any expansion of their own knowledge. Indeed there may be little need really to understand the mathematical background so long as the teacher is prepared simply to follow the instructions. While this could give teachers confidence in using one of these schemes, others might find it inhibiting.

Some schemes are likely to be less inhibiting, but also much less useful in the design of effective curricula simply because they provide only a small amount of information about curricular organisation, compared to the aforementioned schemes. *Peak*, for example, despite being very colourful and attractive, offers relatively little information which can be used as a basis for teaching. Similarly, *Mastermaths* and *Maths Adventure* offer only the briefest set of notes to expand on the content of each page.

A particularly interesting situation arises with the card-based system, *SMP*. With this scheme very brief Teacher's Handbooks and Answer Books are provided for each Unit. They are easy to read but contain only the minimum of advice about teaching, apart from a few lines of advice about classroom organisation and lists of the cards and topics to be used. Probably because the sequence of activities is so strictly defined in the numbering of the children's work cards, little or no advice is offered about how to teach a topic. Indeed it is possible to assume that the material on the work cards is sufficient in itself and that the scheme is therefore 'teacher-proof'. This was probably not the intention of the authors, but the scheme has perhaps tended to become an example of the way in which materials designed to be a flexible tool for the teacher in fact impose an organisational straitjacket.

The question of management and organisation of the scheme in use is therefore a crucial part of decision making at both the planning and purchasing stages as well as in the on-going maintenance of the mathematics curriculum. Such issues as the use of the scheme in various types of classroom organisation and grouping; the problems of curricular continuity and consistency from infant to junior departments or from class to class; the possibilities for modification of the scope, sequence and pace of progress to meet the needs of individual differences; the need to mark effectively children's work, record progress and to produce or select additional materials are all factors which must be considered. At the very least some account must be taken of the demands on the teacher's time and abilities imposed by the various organisational and educational requirements of the scheme.

Almost all the schemes which have been considered in this book claim that they can be used flexibly in a variety of classroom organisations including individual work, group work or class teaching. In the hands of a gifted teacher this may well be true but for the majority of us it is likely that we feel most comfortable with a particular style of classroom organisation and therefore should really be looking at schemes to see whether one or another best fits our particular circumstances.

A case in point is that of *SMP*. The Teacher's Handbook (page 8) states: 'Although SMP 7–13 is mainly individualised, it is possible and desirable to include group work and *ocasional situations* [my emphasis] where the class works as a whole. Some teachers will prefer to have only part of the class working on mathematics at one time, thereby lessening the demand on certain cards and apparatus, other teachers will prefer to have all the class on mathematics.' It also states that 'ideally the cards should be divided up and placed in convenient wall pockets around the room'. If used in the way suggested the type of classroom organisation is likely to be firmly fixed in this flexible, child-centred mode. However, it would be equally possible, although it is not openly stated, for the teacher to use the set of cards in a Module to form the basis of his or her teaching, and only allow children access to the cards (individually or in groups) when the 'teaching', introductory activities and discussion have been completed. Unfortunately, this possible increase in flexibility is not mentioned in the materials for teachers and has been ignored by teachers and many advisers. For some teachers their role specifically as teachers of mathematics has become merely one of supplying resources and marking work cards, with only brief discussion with children allowed because of constraints of time.

On the other hand, *IMP*, published much later than *SMP*, emphasises particularly the need for 'teaching' and 'discussion' and clearly states that cards are used to consolidate and extend learning, rather than being the means of teaching and learning.

Having claimed that their own materials are capable of flexible use in individual work, group work, and class teaching, most authors and publishers then devalue their own claim by attempting to lay clear emphasis on group work, offering advice of variable quality about how it can be organised in relation to the particular scheme. This last proviso is essential because authors clearly vary in their beliefs about the constituents of 'the groups' and how they might be taught.

For example, *Mathematics For Schools* states:

> We strongly advise that classes should be arranged in groups of like ability. Time does not permit you to carry out the necessary introductory activities and discussion with each child working individually. Neither is it usual to find a whole class working appropriately at the same level. Nevertheless there are some children who have to be taught as individuals ... and there are some occasions when it is appropriate to work with a whole class.

The Teacher's Resource Book also suggests a group size of about nine or ten children, working on mathematics while the rest work on 'other' (unspecified) activities, for about 20 minutes for each group. The group then goes on to the practice time which may not require direct involvement of the teacher. *Ginn* and *Arnold Junior Mathematics*, however, broaden this to suggest smaller groups and suggest two methods. In one method all the children in the class progress through the programme at the same rate. New concepts and topics are introduced by class teaching and children then divide into ability groups to continue practical work before moving on to the pupil materials. It is then intended that the more able children go on to enrichment work.

In the second suggested method each group is allowed to progress at its own rate. In this model the opportunities for class teaching becoming increasingly rare, the administration becomes more complicated and it is possible that speed of progress can begin to be emphasised at the expense of deeper understanding and broader experience. The schemes are therefore quite clearly broadly recommending the former method, although allowing for other possibilities. Interestingly, the schemes makes no real mention of individualisation and indeed *Arnold Junior Mathematics* states that it 'is not really designed for fully individualised work' because of the importance of discussion.

Macmillan Junior Mathematics, *Beta* and *Mastermaths* provide only brief information about the possibilities (and problems) of organisation. The suggestions are couched in general terms and are unlikely to be of specific help when organising the particular scheme in question. Clearly, the choice of a scheme could well depend on the amount of help needed by the teachers in a particular school and this is a function of their previous experience of different modes of working. Certainly the change from a scheme orientated towards large groups to, for example, the very individualised nature of *SMP* would require great care because of the major organisational upheaval and adjustments required by the (real or apparent) increase in flexibility of use of the materials.

Similarly, a change from a compact textbook-based scheme like *Beta*, or *Maths Adventure*, to a scheme which provides a large number of peripherals such as worksheets, work cards, activity packs, computer software, black-line masters for photocopying, and spirit duplicator masters and other items would require wholesale changes of attitude and organisational skill on the part of the teachers involved.

Whereas *Beta* or *Maths Adventure* would, in the teacher's notes, merely suggest the need for further practice or an extension/enrichment activity, the schemes like *Ginn* or *SPMG* or *Nuffield* actually provide large amounts of materials which have been clearly linked with particular stages and needs. Note however that the provision of such materials does not imply that they are of good or useful quality.

The less comprehensive schemes (at least in terms of the quantity of resources) therefore place the onus for preparation of materials firmly in the hands of the teacher. Given the current emphasis on practical work, problem-solving and investigational work this can place a severe additional burden on teachers using such schemes and make it virtually impossible for them to meet the demands of modern mathematical education. On the other hand they can always use the increasing range of purposeful supplementary and enrichment materials becoming available. A selection of these is listed at the end of this book.

The point is that effective teaching, whether based on charisma or sheer hard work, is worth a thousand bits of paper, and the vast quantity of material provided by such schemes as *Ginn Mathematics*, *SPMG*, *Nuffield*, and increasingly *Peak* can place an equally severe burden on teachers by the need to store, maintain and co-ordinate the effective use of these resources, particularly since most of them are in worksheet or work card form. In the minds of some teachers flexibility may arise from being able to find their own way to effective teaching using simpler materials. For others, the large range of materials in a single comprehensive scheme, not all of which could possibly be completed by the vast majority of children, provides a greater flexibility of choice of approaches and content and is therefore more useful.

Clearly one person's meat is another person's poison and flexibility (or the lack of it) of content, approach and use of materials can be a major factor affecting the continuity of the curriculum from stage to stage and also the consistency between groups and classes which are notionally working at the same level. Most schemes are designed to provide a progression of skills and knowledge which should be adhered to for effective learning to take place. Clearly, the greater the autonomy afforded to individual teachers, and the greater the allowance for individual differences in children's learning style, intelligence, linguistic competence and motivation, the more difficult it will be for continuity and consistency to be achieved. If continuity and consistency of curriculum are important aims of school management, and it seems likely that they are in the minds of both the higher and lower ranks of the profession, then the choice of a scheme can be crucial to the achievement of these aims.

Within the limits of age and ability specified by the authors of a scheme there is, in general terms, a large measure of built-in consistency and continuity and to a large degree a logical cohesion of style and technique. However, consistency and continuity will really only be achieved if the scheme is rigidly adhered to.

The only other alternative would be for the staff of a school to produce a policy and an independent syllabus for mathematics education which would be sufficiently detailed to allow the use of more than one scheme and the need for continuity and consistency would thus be catered for in a particular school. In fact this may well be the correct way in which to ensure effective mathematical education for children, but it is a daunting task, both for the providers of resources and in terms of record keeping. The important point is to consider schemes which will have already done the bulk of the work for the school by providing materials which cover the needs of many age groups and which allow for different rates of progress and styles of learning.

Some schemes handle the issue by providing materials to cover the whole primary and middle school age range. Examples are *Mathematics For Schools*, *Peak*, *Step by Step* and *Nuffield*. However, it is interesting to note that the first two of these include a textbook known as 'Book O', which provides a revision link between the Infant work for ages 5 to 7 and the Junior/Middle work for ages 7 to 13 to take account of the needs of schools which cater only for a section of the age group.

Other publishers have opted for separate schemes for the different age groups. Among others, Schofield and Sims produce *Time For Maths* for the age range 5 to 7, *Ready For Alpha and Beta* as a link book at the age of 7, and *Alpha* and *Beta* for children aged 7 to 13. The scheme is interesting if only for the fact that the junior and middle school materials are split into *Alpha Mathematics* for children of 'good average and above average ability', and *Beta Mathematics* for children of average and below average ability.

Bell and Hyman offer *Kites* for 5 to 7 year olds and *Maths Adventure* for 7 to 12 year olds. Arnold offer *Moore's Maths For Infants* for 5 to 7 year olds and *Arnold Junior Mathematics* for 7 to 11 year olds. Cambridge University Press offer *IMP* for children aged 5 to 7 and *SMP* for children aged 7 to 13. Macmillan offer *Macmillan Mathematics* for children aged 5 to 8 and *Macmillan Junior Mathematics* for children aged 7 to 11. In these cases there has been close collaboration between the designers of the two schemes and the work flows easily from one to the other. Others may be less effectively linked. Unless links are clearly specified, or implied by common authorship, it is not possible to assume a valid link and other combinations may be more effective for a particular school, such as *Mathematics For Schools* for infants and *SMP* for the junior age groups.

A particular problem, for which a large measure of clearly defined progression coupled with potential or actual flexibility of classroom organisation is essential, is that of catering for children with individual differences in learning style, intelligence, linguistic competence and motivation. One possible response – that of placing children in groups –

is already offered by most of the schemes, but it is a general principle under which to operate, rather than a set of specific guidelines. However, within the groups there will be individual differences and it is necessary to examine the extent to which the various schemes are capable of being modified in terms of scope, sequence and pace to meet the needs of individuals.

An overtly individualised scheme like *SMP* would seem to be capable of effective 'personalisation' by a teacher to fit individual needs. Because the material is arranged in modules a simple removal of certain modules or cards will reduce the quantity of the material and therefore the scope. Conversely, transfer of modules from later units will increase the scope. Within a module the sequence is clearly laid out by the numbering of the cards, but the judicious use of a pair of scissors or sticking labels over the numbers can easily alter the sequence, although care must be taken by the teacher to know what the modified sequence involves. Being individualised the pace can be determined by the use of supplementary devices and materials at the discretion of the teacher.

By their nature, textbook-based schemes are significantly less capable of modification of scope and sequence. In some, like *Racing To Maths*, *Beta*, *Maths Adventure* and *Macmillan Junior Mathematics*, the sequence is quite precisely determined and offers little scope for variation. However, the last two examples do offer some additional sheets and/or cards which, although a part of the scheme, can be used in discretionary ways by the teacher.

The wide range of materials offered by *Ginn Mathematics*, *SPMG* and *Arnold Junior Mathematics* and the early stages of *Step by Step* allow significant alteration of the scope, sequence and pace. However, such modifications are clearly dependent upon the adequate completion of a 'core' of mathematical skills.

Interestingly, no single scheme offers variations in approach to suit different learning styles. Without going into these in detail it is clear that some children learn best from a carefully sequenced set of concepts while others learn more effectively from the use of a problem-solving approach. Any teacher wishing to modify the curriculum on these grounds must really look around for a second scheme or a set of supplementary materials which can be used for this particular and quite common variation within a class.

Two final points are worth a mention in this chapter. The first concerns the possibilities for systematic training of teachers in the use of a particular scheme. It has already been made clear that no two schemes are alike and simple words on a sales handout are not really sufficient, particularly if you are considering one or more of the wide ranging, integrated, multi-level schemes. Specimen copies of materials are always available but some publishers offer a more structured workshop or seminar to introduce the materials. *Nuffield* offer the hire of a video cassette featuring the scheme in use with infants and juniors, and will arrange meetings. *Peak* organises meetings for teachers, often presented by the authors, at which the schemes can be examined. The publishers of *Ginn Mathematics* will arrange displays and demonstrations in schools and Teachers' Centres. However, all publishers are willing to provide a measure of support if a school is considering a particular scheme so that the more overt statements of some publishers should not be taken as meaning that their 'training' will be in any way more effective than the normal provision. Probably the most effective way to learn is to visit a school actually using a scheme and talk to the teachers who are already finding and analysing the problems attached to a particular scheme. Possibly the soundest piece of advice is found in the Teacher's Notes for *Macmillan Junior Mathematics* (page v) where it says 'it

would be advantageous for the head and teachers to familiarise themselves in advance with the pupils' books and the Teacher's Notes'. If that were always done by everyone, staff decision making would be based on effective and real knowledge, and not on hearsay.

'Hearsay' with regard to mathematics is often rife in primary school playgrounds and the need to provide parents (and governors) with information about the content and approach used in the scheme constitutes the final question to be considered. Many schools produce booklets and charts to explain their aims and methods to parents. Clear statements with regard to mathematics are essential. The onus is very much on the schools to conduct their own parent–teacher meetings on curricular matters.

However, two schemes do offer materials specifically for parents. *Mathematics For Schools* produces a Parent's Booklet, sold with the scheme, which outlines the philosophy, content and approaches used. It provides a list of 'dos and don'ts' for parents wanting to help their children's mathematical development. *Nuffield* provides a Parent's Newsletter and suggests that the video mentioned earlier can be used at a PTA meeting. The problem is that while the idea of parent education in these two schemes is sound, the reality is less effective and a school inviting co-operation would need to be much less impersonal and provide information directly related to the particular situation. The gap between publishers' aspirations and classroom reality is often wide and careful reading and sifting of information is essential to valid decision making.

4 *The scheme in relation to children*

However good a scheme may be mathematically, children are unlikely to learn very much from using it unless they understand how it works and what they are supposed to be doing, and unless they can cope with its requirements. Their willingness to do so is likely to be considerably affected by the extent to which they find it attractive, intriguing and relevant to their lives and interests.

Understanding how the scheme works and what is required is of course partly a matter of how the teacher organises and explains it but there may be sign-posting features in the children's materials which make for greater ease or difficulty. It is seldom that these signposts take the form of actual objectives for children to achieve. Their sense of objective has to be based on what teachers say to them, the titles given to the work and the directions, questions or explanations provided in the text.

In the infant schemes or sections of schemes where there tends to be greater reliance on learning experiences organised by the teacher, the children's materials are sometimes envisaged as follow-up work dependent on those experiences and are consequently only minimally signposted. This is the case with *Step by Step* and *Mathematics for Schools*, for example. Where the children's materials are more central to the scheme, it is more likely that titles and headings will be provided. In *IMP*, for example, the separate work books and cards series are clearly labelled as relating to a particular topic such as addition.

With junior materials, children are much more likely to be expected to know what they are doing and where they are going and most children's materials are arranged under headings which indicate the nature of the work. The type of headings used varies enormously from the terse general titles like 'Length' found in *Peak* and *SMP* to the rather more informative titles used in schemes like *Racing to Maths* and the junior materials of *Step by*

Step which give an indication of the type of activity involved. 'Money-subtraction by adding on' (*Racing to Maths C*) or 'Subtraction – counting back on a number line' (*Step by Step*, Flight 2, Level 1 Number Book) give pupils far more orientation to the page or section than simple titles like 'Money'.

Some schemes use non-mathematical titles from time to time. *Kites*, for example, has a sequence of pages entitled 'Nut-eating Weirdies' and *SPMG* a card entitled 'Stick of rock'. The intention presumably is to intrigue children and deliberately to place them in an open situation. It would be important if using a scheme where this occurs to ensure that children were not confused by such titles.

Directions, questions and explanations tend to be minimal in infant materials as the teacher is assumed to provide these verbally. Great reliance is placed on visual indicators. *IMP* Card 1d about weight in Unit 2, for example, shows two children sweating and straining with the effort of handling heavy things. It is common for patterns of work, once having been established to be repeated frequently as in *Kites 2* Number Workbook, pages 3, 4 and 5. Where this is the case, directions may be fuller on the principle that repetition will aid mastery.

Junior materials tend to develop a distinctive directional style which is consistent throughout the age ranges. So *Peak* and *Mastermaths*, for example, adopt a rather terse approach, giving directions such as 'Complete this table' but offering only minimal explanations. *Arnold* and *Ginn* are much more generous in the background information and explanations they offer. Most schemes provide an example of the work children are intended to complete. *Peak* does not necessarily do so.

Information and directions in the children's materials of some schemes seem to be aimed towards the teachers rather than children. This occurs in infant materials in particular (for example *Ginn*, *Racing to Maths*, *SPMG*). But it is also be be found in some junior schemes such as *Mastermaths*. While the appeal seems to be over the heads of the children, it is possible that such a device may also promote clarity in the minds of the more able users.

Most schemes would claim that they provide facilities for individualised learning where this is deemed appropriate but some schemes, for example *Peak* and *SMP*, make this provision a high priority. Others, for example *Arnold* and *Ginn*, emphasise the importance of discussion and collaboration and make group and paired work a high priority. Whatever the claim of a scheme it would, for the most part, be difficult to detect the priorities through an inspection of materials. Peer group co-operation may well be a major aim in a scheme but indications of this in the children's materials tend to be limited to occasional invitations to 'Play this game with a friend' (for example, *Step by Step*) or to 'Work with a friend' (for example, *Ginn*). Individual working is likely to be an assumption unless other conditions are specified and any scheme which offers a good range of materials, particularly card materials, is likely to lend itself to individualised learning. Those which provide branching programmes of reinforcement and enrichment are especially well geared for this but it is interesting to note that two schemes which do this, namely *Ginn* and *Arnold*, are also schemes which value group work and in the case of *Ginn* provide a special basis for it in the form of 'Big Books'.

The reality of the situation is that group work and individual work are by no means mutually exclusive and whatever approach is recommended in a scheme the approach in practice will depend on the extent to which a teacher follows the recommendations rather than on the materials themselves.

It is in the nature of commercially produced schemes that they provide for children in a general sense rather than for special groups of learners. *Racing to Maths* claims that 'the needs of every pupil are met' but more commonly the argument would be that special needs are best catered for by special materials which fall outside the scope of a general scheme. *Peak*, for example, places great emphasis on the need for supplementary materials for children with particular learning difficulties. Where additional materials are provided to help children who experience difficulties, these frequently take the form of extra practice in basic skills, as with *Ginn* and this could be depressing for the children concerned. In *Arnold* there is an attempt to re-present experiences in such a way as to provide a new opportunity for understanding, but frequently in schemes there is little novelty in practice and the activities do not compare well with enrichment activities which tend to be rather more interesting.

The question of motivation is an important one. We know that many children find mathematics difficult and are easily alienated from the subject. This makes it all the more critical that the materials themselves and the activities children are asked to participate in should be such that children involve themselves in mathematics with confidence and enjoyment. But motivation is an elusive quality. It is possible to form a judgement about what is most likely to prove motivating for children but in the event it is a matter of what the individual child conceives of as motivating. All discussions of motivation must take full account of the differences among children and what they view negatively and positively.

Having said that, it is clear that a great deal of thought and ingenuity has gone into devising a style and activities which will appeal to children. Many schemes use comic characters to help promote a sense of fun. Sometimes they appear to be there simply to introduce a note of humour into the task, like the animals who demonstrate the activities at the start of many sections in *Mathematics for Schools*. Sometimes their function is to supply cues and prompts to guide children through the work, like the menagerie of animals scattered through the pages of *Arnold*. Sometimes they embody a particular operation, like *SMP*'s 'Annie Add', said to be 'an engaging character', or a particular approach, like the 'short

Comic characters such as the Short Cut Pig can help children identify an operation or approach. (*Ginn*, Level 5. Textbook 1, p. 37.)

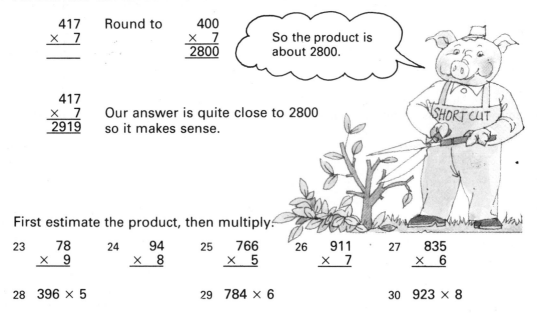

We can use rounding to estimate a product.
An estimate can tell us whether our answer makes sense.

$$\begin{array}{r} 417 \\ \times\ \ 7 \\ \hline \end{array}$$ Round to $$\begin{array}{r} 400 \\ \times\ \ 7 \\ \hline 2800 \end{array}$$ So the product is about 2800.

$$\begin{array}{r} 417 \\ \times\ \ 7 \\ \hline 2919 \end{array}$$ Our answer is quite close to 2800 so it makes sense.

First estimate the product, then multiply.

| 23 | 78 × 9 | 24 | 94 × 8 | 25 | 766 × 5 | 26 | 911 × 7 | 27 | 835 × 6 |

28 396 × 5   29 784 × 6   30 923 × 8

cut' pig in *Ginn*. Other schemes, like *Peak* and *Racing to Maths* decline to indulge in such frivolity.

Constant attention is given to presenting operations in a way which will promote clarity by hooking them on to a concept which children are likely already to possess. The images may be everyday images like frogs jumping or feet walking up steps in the *IMP* work on number sequencing (Unit 1, Workbook 4, page 11) or fantasy images as with the *Mastermaths* number machine (Book 4, page 11). Indeed, the number processing machine seems widely to be considered a potent image as it appears in several of the schemes.

Attractive activities are frequently introduced to sugar the pill of number work. The *Mathematics for Schools* dot-to-dot drawing to develop ordering of numbers (Level 1, Book 5, page 7), and the *Arnold* code work involving addition (Stage 1, Card 63E) are typical examples and again these are common to several schemes. Most schemes appear to appreciate the importance of practice exer-

cises although the amount of space given to these varies. In *Beta*, they constitute the major part of the scheme whereas in *Nuffield* they play only a minor role. Practice exercises can, of course, become tedious and time-consuming for children yet schemes are in general surprisingly unconcerned to raise interest in the work by setting challenges or varying the task. The *Ginn* feature 'Keeping skills sharp' is a step in this direction but the general instruction to 'Copy and complete' which appears in so many schemes (for example *SMP*, *Mastermaths*) seems almost to anticipate tedium.

Many of the most appealing activities proposed in schemes are either dependent on the teacher organising them outside the mainstream materials in response to advice in the teachers' books or reserved for the more able children through an enrichment programme. If the teacher is not prepared to organise practical activities or the children never reach the stage of being 'enriched', the practice of mathematics might be much duller than the description of a scheme suggests so it is important to examine the scheme as a whole rather than simply in terms of activities which may be peripheral.

Many of the infant schemes or sections of schemes rely on an approach which enables children to learn through play. Again, it would be possible for teachers to ignore the advice offered and to confine activities to the core children's materials. Where a scheme actually provides the means of setting play activities in motion, this is less likely to happen. The materials which accompany *IMP* and *Step by Step*, for example, are bold and brightly coloured and the games, rhymes and activities for which they form the basis are likely to prove extremely attractive learning experiences for children.

It is especially important that children should not become anxious about mathematics and one of the greatest advantages in using a scheme may be that as it becomes familiar it provides a feeling of security. If the scheme is well organised, children will known what they have to do and will work with confidence. Children are likely to take comfort from the 'You need' features in *SMP* and *Mastermaths* which ensures that they are prepared for their work. They are likely to find the broken page approach of *Step by Step* and *Mastermaths* reassuring since they are only ever asked to do things a little at a time.

They may also especially appreciate the clarity with which certain schemes indicate what to do next. Some signal the point at which new work is commencing for which they have not been prepared and where they will need to seek their teacher's help. This is particularly clear in *Step by Step* and *Mathematics for Schools*. *Arnold* has a system for indicating which piece of work to undertake next and *SPMG* provides directions for both further work and teacher consultation.

Measures such as these can help give a feeling of security to children using a scheme by helping them to know where they are and what they need to do. But, fundamentally it is the operations children are asked to perform and the connections which are established with their existing understanding which will tend to promote either confidence or anxiety. Such matters have been discussed in the 'Scope and Sequence' section.

There is a noticeable concern in modern schemes to place the work in contemporary settings. References to space, to pop music and to currently popular sports abound and figure largely in illustrations. *Peak's* sharp photographs are particularly effective in establishing a contemporary 'look' although the dangers of ageing are already evident: Gladys Knight and the Pips, for example, are less popular than they were (Book 3, page 13). There is also a determined appeal to the concerns of childhood. *Ginn*, for example, sets a series of questions against the background of a fair (Level 5, Textbook 1, page 40). Many problems involve the buying of toys, the reading of comics and the eating of sweets.

The aim is generally to present universal images of childhood which do not relate to any particular section of society. The illustrations tend to confirm this by portraying children dressed in a style which could be found amongst children in any area in the country, by introducing cartoon-style characters like distracted academics and amiable pirates and by frequent use of animals. *Nuffield* goes further by creating an almost culture-free setting which relates to childhood situations but in depersonalised terms.

The major exception to this trend to generality is a desire to represent ethnic minority groups in the schemes. There is evidence in most schemes of a sensitivity to this issue although the solution sometimes goes no further than the colouring in of a small proportion of the faces (for example, *Mathematics for Schools*). *Peak* and *Ginn* show rather more commitment by presenting both group and individual photographs of children of races other than white British and *Arnold* is one of the few schemes to use appropriate names. The balance of representation is something which is important for all schools but is of particular personal importance in schools where a high proportion of children are from ethnic minorities.

The image of a classless and contemporary society conveyed in illustrations such as these ensure a general appeal. (*Peak* Book 4, p. 57.) (*Peak* Book 5, p. 5.)

Estimate the weight of 6 friends.
Weigh them.
Record your results in a table.

Name	Estimate	Weight

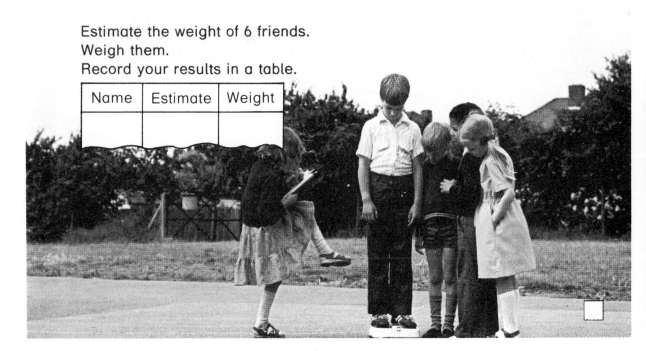

All schools, whatever their location, are likely to have equal numbers of boys and girls and here, too, the balance of representation in schemes is important. Most modern schemes show an awareness of this. It is not just a matter of counting up the number of male and female figures represented, however, although even at this level *Mastermaths*, where the characters are almost exclusively male, could be considered unacceptable. It is also a matter of what the male and female characters do. It is unfortunate, for example, that the teacher figure in *Arnold* is always male and that the glamorous, all-knowing figures in the later units of *SMP* also tend to be male. Subliminal messages conveyed by such stereotypes may contribute to the feelings of inadequacy which girls are prone to develop in the area of mathematics.

It is certainly the case that almost all schemes do make strenuous efforts to ensure that the materials are comprehensible, attractive and motivating and that as much as possible is done to carry children through difficult learning by presenting it in a setting which will appeal. Most children would enjoy the full-colour pictures in *Ginn*, the glossy photographs in *Peak* and the animal characters in *Arnold*. But there are others who will enjoy the relatively sophisticated appeal of *Mastermaths*, the lively, sectionalised approach of *Step by Step*, the bite-sized portions of *SMP* or the stimulus of working 'off the page' which arises with *Nuffield*. The important thing is to match the scheme to the children, not just on the basis of initial appeal but also of long-term use. The pattern of activities that children actually become involved in as a result of working with the scheme will influence motivation long after they have ceased to notice its appearance.

Motivation may be increased by the use of settings which appeal to children's interests. (*Ginn*, Level 5, Textbook 1, pp. 40 and 41.)

Problem solving.

1 Janet went on the Roller Coaster 4 times. How much did she spend on Roller Coaster tickets?

2 How much do 5 Roundabout tickets cost?

3 What is the total cost of 2 rides on the Whip and 2 rides on the Bumper Cars?

4 What is the total cost of 3 Big Wheel rides and 2 Flying Saucer rides?

5 What is the cost of 2 rides on the Waltzer and 3 rides on the Ghost Train?

6 How much would you have left from £2.50 if you had 3 rides on the Roundabout and 1 on the Roller Coaster?

7 How much would you have left from £5.00 after 6 rides on the Flying Saucer?

8 Which costs more, 5 tickets for the Whip or 6 tickets for the Big Wheel?

TICKETS	
Roundabout	45p
Roller Coaster	85p
Big Wheel	55p
Whip	60p
Flying Saucer	40p
Bumper Cars	75p
Ghost Train	35p
Waltzer	45p

9 Which costs more, 4 Ghost Train tickets or 3 Waltzer tickets?

10 Ruth had £3.40. She bought 2 Bumper Car tickets. How much money did she have left?

11 Gary bought 3 Roller Coaster tickets. He gave the ticket seller £3.00. How much change did he get back?

12 Paula had £5.00. She bought 2 Waltzer tickets and 1 Roller Coaster ticket. How much money did she have left?

13 Jason got £5.00 for his birthday. He wanted to go on each ride once. Did he have enough money?

14 Barry had £2.05. He went on the Roundabout twice and the Bumper Cars once. What other rides could he go on?

keeping skills sharp

Complete these to make the fractions equivalent.

15 $\frac{1}{2} = \frac{}{6}$

16 $\frac{4}{4} = \frac{}{3}$

17 $\frac{1}{3} = \frac{}{9}$

18 $\frac{3}{2} = \frac{}{4}$

19 $\frac{5}{6} = \frac{}{12}$

20 $\frac{3}{5} = \frac{}{10}$

21 $\frac{2}{3} = \frac{}{12}$

22 $\frac{3}{4} = \frac{}{12}$

5 Language

Detailed study of the relationship between language and thought, language and conceptual development, and language and problem-solving ability are beyond the scope of this book. Readers are referred to Section 4 of Dickson, L. *et al.*, *Children Learning Mathematics*, Holt Education (1984); and Shuard, H. and Rothery, A., *Children Reading Mathematics*, John Murray (1984) if they wish to extend their study of the more subtle aspects of language mentioned in the schedule for analysing published materials and schemes. Similarly, attempts to make valid assessments of readability through the calculation of reading ages are fraught with conceptual and logistical difficulties to the point where the exercise becomes rather aimless and has indeed been omitted from our analysis of the schemes. Nevertheless there are a number of opportunities for informal observation and consideration of the quality of the attempts made by authors of schemes to provide an appropriate input of language to a scheme.

The essential points are that a child should first, *with appropriate teaching*, be able to read the instructions, hints and conclusions offered in the pupils' books. Secondly, and again *with appropriate teaching*, the child should be able to develop understanding of the peculiarities and subtleties of mathematical language.

At the simplest level this process is aided by the clarity of the chosen print size and typeface, combined with general page layout and design. Slightly more dependent on the teacher's skill is the use of diagrams, subheadings, symbols, signals, prompts and hints to help the child to develop his or her ability to work independently. While these are important it cannot be stressed enough that for children to 'read' mathematics adequately they must be *taught* to do so, rather than left to 'pick up' language as it arises. This is achieved partly by the use of correct terminology in the pupils' books and by attempts to avoid convoluted instructions or excessively pedantic grammar in page design, but also by the provision of clear advice about vocabulary in the materials provided for teachers.

The Cockcroft Report (1982) stressed the importance of discussion and the child's use of verbal, written, symbolic and diagrammatic forms of communication. It is therefore important that the choice of a scheme should currently place emphasis on discussion and a developing confidence, on the part of the pupil, to talk confidently about mathematical ideas and then set them down in a more permanent, but still meaningful, way.

Many of the more recent schemes claim a particular concern to keep the reading demands of the children's materials within the capacities of the target age group. In *Ginn Mathematics*, for example, language is therefore kept within strict limits in the work books and in the textbooks, although becoming, quite rightly, more sophisticated in the enrichment work cards. Technical language is introduced where appropriate but teachers are alerted to the vocabulary demands at each stage and, if they prepare children by careful exposition and discussion as suggested, the children should have no difficulties with the text. The teacher's own understanding of mathematical terms is aided by the inclusion of both a glossary and a vocabulary list at the end of each book.

The children's materials are clearly set out and the relatively neat and uncluttered appearance of the pages is likely to make them attractive and approachable by the children. Consistent visual themes appear throughout the scheme to serve as an instant key to procedures. Headings, clear 'reminders', arrow indicators, and prompts are used to advantage. Discussion between teacher and children is one of the stated tenets of the scheme. The 'Big Book' system is a sound vehicle for promoting this. However, there is little indication of provision for discussion among children, although this will occur incidentally in the course of using the enrichment cards, assuming they are used.

Mathematics For Schools is particularly concerned with the use of correct mathematical language. Glossaries and vocabulary lists are included and many opportunities for discussion are highlighted in the Teacher's Resource Books and the pupils' materials. A variety of visual signals are used throughout the scheme. Particularly useful ones are the 'Stop' signal, the 'Game' signal and the 'Spirit Master' signal, each of which directs the child back to the teacher for advice and guidance. *Mathematics For Schools* is very 'mathematical' in style and use of terminology, insisting that all children, including the very youngest, should use the correct terminology.

A card-based and individualised system like *SMP*, and the infant level *IMP*, has necessitated great care being taken over the provision of clear language. In general, explanations and instructions must be, and are, simple and straightforward. On the whole the correct mathematical terms are used (with the possible exception of the use of the term 'weight' rather than 'mass' – although schemes seem to be divided on the extent to which they should be mathematically pure on this topic). However, reinforcement of the use of terms, and even the pronunciation of words, is left to the child unless the teacher examines this aspect while marking and discussing the work done. The Teacher's Handbook lists 'new' terms used and, if we assume that the handbook is in constant use, then a measure of discussion and reinforcement of correct language is likely.

In fact once children have become used to the style of working semi-independently with a work card system there should be few problems with language. Only children with severe reading problems are likely to find difficulty. This is generally a result of children looking for 'sums' rather than regarding the cards as guides to mathematical activity. Again the onus is on the teacher to make effective use of the materials.

In general the cards are clearly designed with good quality print. The artwork in *SMP* is at times excessively distorted and stylised but spacing is effective, diagrams are well drawn and good use is made of the two-colour printing. An interesting point is that many of the cards at all levels would be useful for the purpose of stimulating discussion, but this possibility is neither written into the cards nor effectively mentioned in the Handbooks. Clearly, significant amounts of teacher preparation and extension would be required if children were to develop the ability to talk confidently about mathematics.

Almost the exact opposite of *SMP* is the *Beta* scheme. *Beta* does not make particularly heavy demands on the reading ability of children. Words are simple, sentences and paragraphs are short and the vocabulary is undemanding. However, some questions are stated in formal and correct grammatical form which is likely to make them less easy to understand for a child with underdeveloped language skills.

It is emphasised frequently in the teacher's notes that every topic must be introduced by the teacher and this procedure may well forestall any difficulties in the introduction of new vocabulary or subject matter. As has been found with other schemes the onus is on the teacher to introduce, explain and develop the use of mathematical language. There is no such thing as a teacher-proof mathematics scheme!

The main problem with a scheme like *Beta* is that it does not properly encourage discussion of mathematical thinking. Since conversation is likely to play only a small part in the children's experience, if this scheme is used it is unlikely that they will develop the confidence to talk about mathematical ideas. Conversation could well stay at the level of 'Please, Miss, is this right?' As a question this is quite valid. However, the quality of the teacher's response is crucial to develop learning, and the materials offered in this scheme do little to help the teacher to stretch children's learning by suggesting positive ways to answer that question.

It is clear that the quality of the language

built into the schemes, and likely to be generated by the schemes, is extremely variable. Despite the recommendations of the Cockcroft Report and various papers produced by Her Majesty's Inspectorate which encourage language development across the curriculum, a teacher may well feel that he or she can handle the language without a great deal of help from the scheme. If that is so then the range of possible schemes to be chosen is wide and the published materials become a mere tool to support the skill and creativity of the teacher.

On the other hand, it is possible that a teacher may be unsure about his or her own knowledge of mathematics. That being so the maximum amount of support and clarity is essential. The choice is then narrowed greatly to those which have made clearly defined and recognisable efforts to control the language input while simultaneously developing greater language output. In the final analysis the choice depends on the needs of the teacher and the school, and should be an essential ingredient in the process of decision-making.

6 *Assessment and record keeping*

Assessment

Nearly all modern schemes make some provision for assessment. At infant level it is likely to be in the form of advice to monitor work constantly. The teacher's involvement in children's activities is assumed to give him or her a clear picture of how individual children are progressing. This is the basis recommended in *Ginn*, *Step by Step*, *Peak* and *Macmillan Mathematics*, for example. Some schemes make specific suggestions in the teachers' books about how this can be done, *Ginn* recommending informal testing activities and *Mathematics for Schools* providing 'check-ups', lists of questions, requiring an oral or practical response from the child. The process of continuous assessment is aided in *Peak* by the provision of assessment workbooks and in *Macmillan Mathematics* by 'check' cards, a series of problem collections based on preceding work cards. An assessment workbook is also provided for the *Alpha* and *Beta Mathematics* schemes to help teachers to decide on which scheme would be appropriate for children at first year junior level.

These measures are designed to assist the teacher in evaluating a child's progress without putting the child into a situation of possibly threatening formality. At junior level, *Nuffield* continues to rely on constant teacher monitoring and shows little interest in regular progress testing but in this respect it differs from most other schemes where assessment is more likely to take the form of regular tests. These may be included in the children's core textbook materials as is the practice in *Peak* and *Beta*, or in workbooks (for example *Arnold*) or as spirit masters (for example *Ginn*). The degree of regularity can vary considerably, however, from a single section at the end of a book (*Beta*) to a progress check after most topics (*Step by Step*) or Unit sections (*SMP*). Occasionally the intervals are related to time:

with *Ginn* the tests are geared to each half term and the end of the year. With *Ginn* there is also the helpful feature of parallel forms so that children can be retested at the same level if required. Few schemes provide facilities for a second go, yet if the tests are to be taken seriously, this could be considered an essential element.

Assessment occurs under a variety of names such as 'revision' (*Mastermaths* and *Racing to Maths*), 'mixed problems' (*Arnold*) 'progress checks' (*Step by Step*), 'check-ups' (*Ginn*) and straightforward 'assessment' (*Peak*).

Assessment at junior level tends to be rather more formal than at infant level and because it is generally included as part of the work of the scheme, it is possible for feedback to the child to be immediate. Indeed, in *Beta*, the child is invited to 'Test yourself'. Where assessment is less formal, as is usually the case in infant level schemes, and relies on the teacher's professional judgement, it is less certain that this will be communicated to the children.

Almost all formal assessment is criterion-referenced testing: the writers have decided upon criteria which they consider it important for children to achieve and the test items refer to those criteria, whether they be the ability to add together two numbers of a certain size or the ability to measure a given line.

Progress tests appear in a variety of forms. Most include at least some problem-solving work but the proportion may vary considerably. Sometimes they consist of a mixed bag of mechanical arithmetic and problems (for example *Peak*) and sometimes they are made up entirely of problems (for example *Arnold*). Sometimes they are based directly on the work immediately preceding the test (for example *Step by Step*) and sometimes they range over a variety of work (for example *Ginn*).

One feature that almost all have in common, however, is that they refer quite specifically to the work of the scheme, that is to say, they are tests of what has been taught. Schemes may represent what they are doing as testing 'skills and concepts' (for example *Step by Step* and *Peak*), but in practice the tests tend to stick very closely to the actual content of the schemes, to the subject matter and format of the materials. They also tend to reflect the balance of the schemes. This means that the testing can at best only be as satisfactory as the scheme is; if the scheme is considered to be weak in certain areas the chances are that the testing will be similarly weak. *Beta*, for example, tends to emphasise recall and mastery of processes in its tests just as it does in its books. There is little concern with applications of principles to novel situations or with problem solving. It must be said in fairness, however, that very few of the assessment programmes in the schemes show any concern with testing children's ability to apply what they have learned to new situations even though this may be claimed in the scheme as an important goal. Indeed, *Peak* specifically excludes this, neatly suggesting that it will occur as the child tackles the work in the next book and that in any case teachers can invent their own means of testing for this ability.

SPMG is exceptional in that it is including in its newly devised 'Progress Tests' a section on problem solving which it claims will provide the challenge of unfamiliar situations while *Step by Step* shows an awareness of the difficulty by drawing attention to the fact that success on the test does not guarantee understanding and teachers will need to look for this in the child's day-to-day work.

While the content of tests appears to shadow the content of schemes very closely, there is often considerable divergence between the proposed activity of the scheme and that of the test. In particular, the scheme may lay great store by oral and practical work but the test may require only a pencil and paper response. This is the case with, for example, *Arnold*, *Peak* and *Ginn*. Inevitably, this leaves activities which have been claimed to be important in the schemes completely unsampled in the tests. Laudable attempts to overcome this difficulty have been made in one or two schemes. *Mathematics for Schools* and *SMP*, for example, both include ways of assessing children's oral and practical ability and *SMP* presents some practical problems in the assessment tests. On another dimension, a concern is shown in *Step by Step* for children's ability to perform mental operations at speed and a battery of mental arithmetic tests involving oral presentation is included both to teach and test this ability.

The balance of tests is one which concerns children as well as teachers. Whenever formal testing material is provided the likelihood is that children will obtain quick feedback on their performance and will put their own interpretation on this information. There are dangers as well as virtues in this for the feedback is only as fair as the test and as has already been stated, most tests sample the scheme quite closely. So a child might do badly on *Beta*, for example, and develop a poor image of him/herself as a mathematician but have skills in practical or investigational work which are unsampled by the test. Similarly, a child might do very well on *Peak*, for example, but have only a limited grasp of generalised principles and meet difficulty in applying his/her learning to novel situations. The more immediate feedback is, the more important it is that it should be realistic and, as this may not always be the case with a scheme, care should be taken to ensure that children do not develop a distorted self image.

A series of very important questions which need to be asked about any assessment programme concern its purpose. Teachers need to know what they are testing for and what they might be able to do with the results. At the very least a good assessment programme can be expected to provide illumination: clearly it is a good thing to know where we stand in terms of the progress children are making. But how do we rate that progress? What do we judge to be satisfactory and what gives us cause for concern? How do we know what to do if the progress is poor and how do we know what to do if it is good?

Diagnosis and prescription do not preoccupy the writers of mathematics schemes.

Almost without exception the schemes are disappointing in this respect. It is most unusual to find levels of competence defined and it is left chiefly to a teacher's judgement to decide what is acceptable, what is outstanding and what is unsatisfactory. One of the very few instances where a level is specified is in Book B of *Racing to Maths* where it is suggested that 80 per cent of the revision work 'should be completed correctly to ensure an easy transition to Book C'.

There is also little specific advice about what to do about results. If the teacher judges a child's performance on a test to be good, the only assumption must be that the child should follow the path generally suggested for successful children. They are to be allowed, for example, to 'forge ahead' (*Beta*), undertake 'enrichment work' (*Ginn*) or work on 'extension materials' (*Arnold*). These suggestions are all couched in very general terms and do not relate directly to the tests.

Even more worrying, perhaps, is the lack of clear advice about what to do if a child does badly on a test. Here the particular types and areas of error are likely to be critical and suggestions need to be quite specific as to these but in these cases they are not. Some schemes, for example *Macmillan Junior Mathematics*, *Ginn* and *Arnold*, provide extra materials to 'reinforce', 'give practice' or 'consolidate' the learning of children likely to experience difficulties but these tend to be generalised and again unrelated to test results. Discussions about tests generally bring exhortations to give extra help to the weaker child but very little indication of what that help might be. Indeed, the subject is frequently dismissed with a few generalities such as 'if mistakes arise in the test, care should be taken that they are not due to a lack of understanding of the concepts and skills involved' (*Peak*) or 'appropriate remedial action can then be planned' (*Beta*). This kind of generalised advice is not very helpful to the teacher.

The response to such criticism would doubtless be that children's actual work on the scheme provides a source of continuous assessment and that the teachers' books offer teaching suggestions which can be turned to when things go wrong. There are two respects in which this would not be an entirely satisfactory response. First, if continuous assessment is to be the main means of assessment, there seems little point in making extensive provision for formal tests, particularly as no means of interpreting these tests is provided in the majority of cases. Secondly, the teaching suggestions provided in the teachers' books are substantially first time approaches. Few are strong in providing suggestions for what to do if the first approach fails. *Macmillan Mathematics*, *Nuffield* and *Step by Step* are among the schemes which do pride themselves on this aspect of mathematics teaching but in others the recommendation is distinctly in terms of giving children who have failed more of the same experiences (for example *Ginn*). Teachers who are particularly concerned about this question of helping children with difficulties should go through the teachers' books in some detail to determine the level of guidance offered.

In most schemes, there is no suggestion that the test results should occur as anything other than a single mark. Some schemes, for example *SMP* and *Ginn*, provide space for recording this on a record grid. Facilities are not usually provided for teachers to establish profiles of the children's achievement in mathematics which would help them to plan future work although it is often possible to detect quite easily which bits of the scheme a child is good at, or failing at, and *Ginn* helps to simplify this process by providing indicators for the origin of each test item.

But teachers may want to know more than the pattern of the child's performance on the scheme. They may want to know about strengths and weaknesses in particular areas of content such as money, shape or time. They may want to be able to see how the child performs in each of the four rules of number or how he/she deals with the various measurement systems. Over and above this, they may want to know how the child fares in different types of mathematical activity such as recall of facts, routine skills, or investigations. Most schemes do not provide the facilities for making these kinds of general judgements easily. *Beta* and *Step by Step* do go some way towards it by organising their tests according to content so that it would be possible to devise a profile of performance on the areas specified. But for the most part lack of interest in profiling is in keeping with the self-contained nature of schemes. The tests are tests of performance on the scheme and may not be revealing about general mathematical ability.

Peak is one of the few schemes where sensitivity has been shown to this issue. The scheme is linked to the new NFER standardised tests of mathematics for the junior age range so that teachers can relate their children's performance to national norms and assess their progress in mathematics rather than *Peak*. It would be a wise precaution for any school adopting a scheme not to rely solely on the assessment provided in the scheme but to establish a policy for other testing measures which would overcome the tendency to insularity present in many schemes.

Record Keeping

There is a high level of awareness of the importance of record keeping shown in almost all schemes, but they vary in their solution to the problem that keeping adequate but not overwhelming records poses. Some like *Beta* restrict themselves to exhortations, giving little help in the way of facilities or models. Most provide either facilities for recording or detailed advice about how to establish a system. Essentially two models are proposed.

The first and most frequently proposed model consists of either placing a tick or colouring in a square to indicate that a particular section of the scheme has been completed. Grids are provided for this purpose in many schemes; *Ginn, SMP, SPMG* and *IMP* are examples. Sometimes these are presented in the form of masters for duplication (*Mastermaths*) and sometimes they are a more substantial, separate publication (*Ginn*). There is seldom space for comment about performance or for recording the development of performance over time. The principle is chiefly that of logging the progress of the scheme.

Underlying an apparent similarity of system, considerable differences of purpose in keeping records are implicit. In *Peak*, for example, a record sheet for each child is proposed and the teacher would maintain this as a means of monitoring the child's progress. In *Arnold*, the record sheet has been designed in the form of a snake to be attractive to children with the idea that they should be involved in monitoring their own progress. In *Ginn*, there is a master record sheet for the whole class and the suggestion is made that this should be displayed so that individual progress becomes a matter of public concern.

The second model is that proposed in *Nuffield* and *Step by Step*. It is based on storage of children's work. *Step by Step* provides a wallet for this purpose and incidentally in doing so incorporates the first model by providing a grid detailing the concepts and skills in the relevant pupils' books so that the teacher can signal acquisition on the child's part. It is suggested that the wallet should contain key work, including progress checks, and should accompany the child as he/she makes his/her way through the school. *Nuffield* offers similar advice although it is left to the teacher to provide the folder. Such a system allows work outside the scheme to be included in the record, and may therefore be more useful to the teacher who does not intend to rely exclusively on a single scheme. It is important for teachers to preserve a degree of independence in relation to testing and recording systems for they can become the ties that bind them to a particular scheme. The promotion of testing only what occurs in the scheme and the provision of facilities for recording only what occurs in the scheme encourages the impression that mathematics itself is only what occurs in the scheme.

Recording systems can be fun for children to use themselves. (*Arnold Junior Maths*, Stage 1 Extension and Reinforcement Sheets, Pupil Record Sheet 1.)

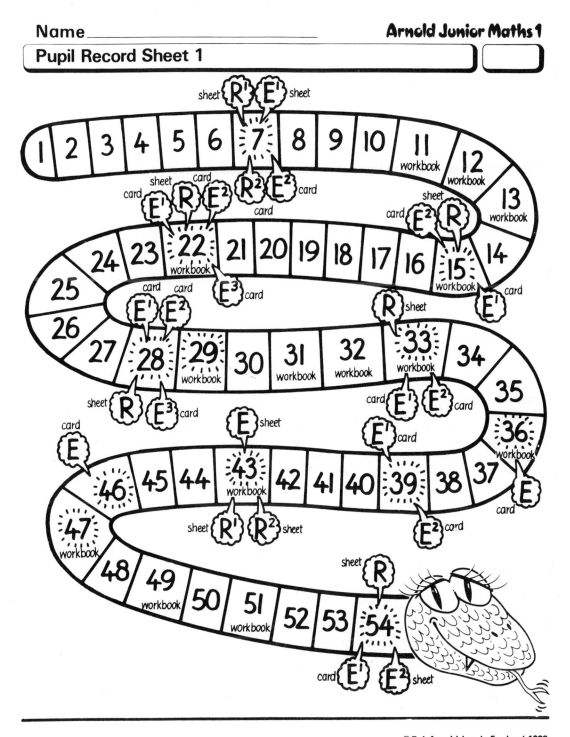

Conclusion

This survey of mathematics schemes is not intended to be comprehensive. It is intended to show how the schedule of questions can be used and in the process to convey something of the flavour of the schemes referred to. One vital element is inevitably missing and this is the school's assessment of a scheme in relation to itself. The whole process of reaching a decision has to begin and end with the school for only if the scheme is well matched to the requirements of the school are the materials likely to be truly assimilated and used with confidence.

The survey shows clearly the variations in quality and emphasis to be found not only amongst schemes but also amongst parts of the same scheme. It reveals many strengths but it also reveals weaknesses and a detailed analysis of any single scheme would doubtless reveal more. Certainly no scheme is without its faults so whatever the choice may be there is likely to be a need to strengthen, to adapt or to supplement the materials. In this context, some flaws may be more worrying than others. It is easier to overcome the difficulties posed by flimsy answer books, for example, than those posed by confusing presentation. Similarly, it may be more feasible to find alternatives for some parts of a scheme than others: just as with reading, it may be easier to

provide alternative extension work than to slot in alternative presentations of basic learning sequences. The degree to which weaknesses are fundamental or peripheral must have a considerable effect on any final judgement about a scheme.

It is hoped that the book will have helped readers develop the habit of looking critically at schemes and that they will extend the technique to any new materials which emerge in the future. If through their own analysis teachers arrive at a position of being able to draw up a shortlist of schemes likely to suit their requirements, it is important that they should visit schools where the schemes can actually be seen in operation and where they can talk to teachers actually using them before any final choice is made. This point has emerged frequently throughout the survey and cannot be emphasised too strongly.

It is perhaps fitting to conclude with a reminder that the final decision may well be that none of the schemes is entirely suitable or that the best balance of materials for a particular situation can be achieved by drawing on the good features of several different schemes. If this should prove to be the case, the time given to examining schemes will have been well spent for the decision will have been made on the basis of evidence rather than intuition.

Major schemes

Title	Publisher	Author	Target Age	Type
Action Mathematics	Cassell	Bass, D. *et al.*	7–11	Mainstream
Alpha Mathematics	Schofield and Sims	Goddard, T. R. *et al.*	7–13	Mainstream
Arnold Junior Maths	Arnold–Wheaton	Various	7–11	Mainstream
Basic Mathematics	Oliver and Boyd	Griffiths, A. L.	7–12	Mainstream
Beta Mathematics	Schofield and Sims	Goddard, T. R. *et al.*	7–13	Mainstream
Ginn Mathematics	Ginn	Various	5–12	Mainstream
Hey Mathematics	Cassell	Various	6–12	Mainstream
Infant Maths Project	Cambridge	Various	5–7	Mainstream
Kent Mathematics Project	Ward Lock Education	Various	8–16	Mainstream
Key Mathematics	Oliver and Boyd	Griffiths, A. L.	5–12	Mainstream
Kites	Bell and Hyman	Stanfield, J.	5–7	Mainstream
Link Mathematics	Cassell	Bass, D. *et al.*	10–13	Mainstream
Macmillan Junior Maths	Macmillan Education	Nolan, M.	7–11	Mainstream
Macmillan Mathematics	Macmillan Education	Snowdon, L.	5–8	Mainstream
Mastermaths	Oxford	Briten, P.	7–11	Mainstream
Mathematics for Schools	Addison–Wesley	Various	5–12	Mainstream
Maths Adventure	Bell and Hyman	Stanfield, J.	7–12	Mainstream
Maths Makes Sense	Arnold–Wheaton	Althans, S. *et al.*	7–12	Mainstream
Moore's Maths for Infants	Arnold–Wheaton	Moore, W.	5–7	Mainstream
Nuffield Maths	Longman	Various	5–11	Mainstream
Numberland	Collins Educational	Edwards, S. *et al.*	4–8	Mainstream
Peak Mathematics	Nelson	Brighouse, A. *et al.*	5–13	Mainstream
Racing to Maths	Hulton	Tansley, A. E. *et al.*	5–12	Mainstream
SPMG	Heinemann Education	Various	5–12	Mainstream
School Maths Project	Cambridge	Various	7–13	Mainstream
Step By Step Mathematics	Blackie	Heron, G. *et al.*	4–13	Mainstream
Target Mathematics	Hulton	Slater, J. D.	7–12	Mainstream
Time for Maths	Schofield and Sims	Goddard, T. R. *et al.*	5–7	Mainstream
Towards Mathematics	Schofield and Sims	Sturgess, D. *et al.*	7–12	Mainstream
A Way With Maths	Cambridge	Langdon, N. *et al.*	10+	Supplementary
Basic 5 to 10 a Day	Oliver and Boyd	Griffiths, A. L.	6–12	Supplementary
Basic Maths	Collins	Hollands, R. *et al.*	7–11	Supplementary
Colouring Puzzles	Longman		6–11	Supplementary
Count and Colour	Oliver and Boyd	Dougall, K. *et al.*	5–7	Supplementary
Early Years Maths Workbooks	Macmillan Education	Dixon, R.	6–8	Supplementary
Everyday Maths	Macmillan Education	Althans, S. *et al.*	7–11	Supplementary
Follow-Up Maths	Oxford	Briten, P.	7–11	Supplementary
Four a Day/Ten a Day	Oliver and Boyd	Griffiths, A. L.	6–12	Supplementary
Impact Maths	Bell and Hyman	Stanfield, J. *et al.*	8–13	Supplementary
Keystrokes	Longman	Griffiths, A. L.	8–13	Supplementary
Let's Solve Problems	Basil Blackwell	Hollands, R.	7–11	Supplementary
Master Your Tables	Basil Blackwell	Millinship, L. P. *et al.*	7–11	Supplementary

Maths Minipacks	Addison–Wesley	Harper, E. *et al.*	8–13	Supplementary
Maths Plus	Ward Lock Education	Harling, P.	7–12	Supplementary
Maths Practice Workbooks	Macmillan Education	Dixon, R.	7–12	Supplementary
Maths Topics	Cassell	Barrett, W. G. *et al.*	7–12	Supplementary
Maths With a Story	Cambridge	Stewart, S.	8–12	Supplementary
Mental Arithmetic	Cassell	Jex, S. F.	8–11	Supplementary
Mental Arithmetic	Schofield and Sims	Goddard, T. R. *et al.*	7–12	Supplementary
More Practice	Schofield and Sims	Adams, J. W. *et al.*	7–12	Supplementary
Nelson Arithmetic	Nelson	Kaner, P.	7–12	Supplementary
Nelson Mental Maths	Nelson	Saunders, J. G.	7–12	Supplementary
Number 1–4	Nelson	Kaner, P.	6–10	Supplementary
Number Practice	Schofield and Sims	Stables, A.	7–11	Supplementary
Number Workbooks	Nelson	Saunder, J. G.	7–11	Supplementary
Odd Minute Maths	Basil Blackwell	Althans, S.	7–11	Supplementary
Oxford Introductory Maths	Oxford	Gregory, O.	5–7	Supplementary
Practice in Basic Skills	Collins	Newton, D. *et al.*	7–11	Supplementary
Practice in Number	Macmillan Education	Cordin, P. W.	7–12	Supplementary
Quicksilver Maths	Basil Blackwell	Wood, A.	7–11	Supplementary
Starting Points	Schofield and Sims	Sims, C. A.	5–7	Supplementary
Steps In Number	Nelson	Saunders, J. G.	5–8	Supplementary
Tables Trail	Longman	Cuff, C.	7–11	Supplementary
Tackling Tables	Cassell	Smith, J.	7–12	Supplementary
The Big Red Bus Series	Arnold–Wheaton	Wood, L. *et al.*	4–7	Supplementary
The Complete Tables Book	Basil Blackwell	Millinship, L. P. *et al.*	7–11	Supplementary
The Number Books	Schofield and Sims	Parker, A. *et al.*	5–7	Supplementary
Think and Solve	Cambridge	Clarke, H. *et al.*	7–12	Supplementary
Workjobs	Addison–Wesley	Baratta-Lorton, M.	5–7	Supplementary

Bibliography

ASSESSMENT OF PERFORMANCE UNIT (1981) *Mathematical Development*, Primary Surveys 1 and 2. London: HMSO.

BELL, A. W., COSTELLO, J. and KUCHEMANN, D. E. (1983) *A Review of Research in Mathematics Education. Part A: Research on Learning and Teaching.* Windsor: NFER/Nelson.

DEPARTMENT OF EDUCATION AND SCIENCE (1965) *Mathematics in Primary Schools.* Schools Council Curriculum Bulletin No. 1. London: HMSO.

DEPARTMENT OF EDUCATION AND SCIENCE (1978) *Primary Education in England.* London: HMSO.

DEPARTMENT OF EDUCATION AND SCIENCE (1979) *Mathematics from 5–11.* London: HMSO.

DEPARTMENT OF EDUCATION AND SCIENCE (1980) *A View of the Curriculum.* London: HMSO.

DEPARTMENT OF EDUCATION AND SCIENCE (1982) *Mathematics Counts* (The Cockcroft Report), London: HMSO.

DEPARTMENT OF EDUCATION AND SCIENCE (1985) *Mathematics for 5 to 16.* London: HMSO.

DICKSON, L., BROWN, M. and GIBSON, O. (1984) *Children Learning Mathematics.* London: Holt, Rinehart and Winston.

EGGLESTON, S. J. (1983) *Learning Mathematics.* APU Occasional Paper No. 1. London: DES.

HARLING, P. (1979) 'Choosing Texts for Primary School Mathematics', *Mathematics in Schools, 8*, 4.

LUMB, D., ELLIS, R. D., ROBERTS, H. and ROBINSON, R. E. (1984) *Primary Maths: A Critical Appraisal Instrument.* London: Longman.

LUNZER, E. and GARDNER, K. (eds) (1979) *The Effective Use of Reading.* London: Heinemann.

SHUARD, H. and ROTHERY, A. (eds) (1984) *Children Reading Mathematics.* London: John Murray.

Acknowledgments

The authors and publishers would like to thank the following for permission to reproduce the following material in this book:
Unwin Hyman for the extract from Book 4 of *Maths Adventure* on p. 54; Arnold-Wheaton for the extract from *Arnold Junior Maths* on p. 79; Longman for the extract from *Nuffield Maths 1 Teachers' Handbook*, General Editor: E. A. Albany, Editor: W. Moore on p. 37; Thomas Nelson and Sons Ltd for the extracts from *Peak Mathematics* on p. 68; Cambridge University Press for the Card 1d from *IMP* on p. 35; Ginn and Company Ltd for the extracts from *Ginn Mathematics*, Level 5, Textbook 1 on p. 66 and pp. 70–71.
Text photos by Sally & Richard Greenhill.

Index